TEATIME TALES
FROM DUNDEE

Also by Maureen Reynolds

Voices in the Street
The Sunday Girls
Towards a Dark Horizon
The Sun Will Shine Tomorrow

TEATIME TALES FROM DUNDEE

New Journeys Down Memory Lane

Maureen Reynolds

Black & White Publishing

First published 2009
by Black & White Publishing Ltd
29 Ocean Drive, Edinburgh EH6 6JL

1 3 5 7 9 10 8 6 4 2   09 10 11 12 13

ISBN: 978 1 84502 249 5

A CIP catalogue record for this book is available
from the British Library.

Typeset by RefineCatch Limited, Bungay, Suffolk
Printed and bound by Scandbook A/B, Sweden

Contents

1

Street Games with Wallace Beery

If I have an abiding memory of the seven-week school holiday it is playing on the streets of Dundee. Pouring out of school on the last week of June was similar to escaping from prison. The feeling of joy and childish exuberance at the thought of an eternity of freedom was indescribable.

The streets, which were noisy at the best of times, were suddenly abuzz with the shouts and laughter from hordes of children.

The boys played 'Pinner', a game that seemed to consist of small pieces of metal being thrown down on the ground. As to the intricacies of this game, I'm afraid the rules escaped me at the time and the years haven't improved my grasp of the game.

Football with a tiny, cheap ball was another favourite, as was a great deal of jostling, wrestling and jersey pulling. Chalking up wickets on a wall and playing cricket almost started World War III when the chalk mark on the ball was hotly disputed.

'Eh telling you. The ba' hit the wicket.'

Unlike real cricket stumps, which were knocked over when hit, our chalked version remained solidly on the wall.

Then there were the 'Pilers'; homemade carts made from empty boxes and four wheels, usually old pram wheels. Dundee, being built on a hill was a great place for scooting down braes with nothing more scientific than a piece of Mum's washing rope to guide the wheels, and a good pair of strong sandals to act as a brake.

Playing 'Chuckies' was another popular pastime. A pile of small stones was placed on the back of the hand and with a quick flick of the wrist the player had to catch the stones in his palm. This went on until there were no stones left.

In my opinion, however, the girls had the best games. Stotting a ball was universally popular and the streets resounded to high-pitched chants of:

One, two, three, O'Leary.
Eh saw Wallace Beery.
Sitting on his bum-ba-leerie.
Eating chocolate soldiers.

Then there was the ball in the stocking or long sock. My cousins recall playing this game. With each strike on the wall, the stocking got longer and longer. Each convoluted movement was accompanied by:

Stot, stot, ba', ba'.
Twenty lassies at the wa'.
No a lad among them a'.
Stot, stot, ba', ba'.

Skipping with a rope was another pastime. The

number of different manoeuvres needed was something that only girls could get the hang of. I have to admit that I enjoyed the more gentler rope games and not 'Firies', where the vicious *swish swish* of the rope was so hard that it sounded like a whip striking the road. Some girls were able to jump in and out as the rope whirled around them. How they didn't lose an eye or have a whiplash to their faces was always a mystery to me.

Playing 'Boxies', or hopscotch as it was known in polite circles, was also a great way to spend a whole day. Chalking on the pavements and skimming empty shoe-polish tins towards the squares took a lot of concentration, as did the hopping, jumping and turning, because this game called for a balancing act – again, best suited to girls.

Both boys and girls played 'Kick the Can'. In fact if you had a big, burly lad on your team who also owned a pair of tough tacketty boots, then you were made. As he lined up to take an almighty wallop, and if his aim was good, then the can would maybe reach the junction of the street and the Hilltown, where it would roll down the brae. With twenty whooping kids running off to find hiding places before the can was retrieved, it was maybe just as well that there was little traffic on the roads.

Later, when tired of running up and down after an old can, we would all gather in a line, arms held above our heads in an arch and sing:

The big ship sails through the alley, alley O,
The alley, alley O, the alley, alley O.

Oh the big ship sails through the alley, alley O
On a cold and frosty morning.

As the song progressed, a line of kids would go under
one of the arches and, at the end of the game, we all
stood with our arms crossed over our chests.

How well I remember the year of the paper parasols. I don't know who started the trend but in a
couple of days nearly every girl in the surrounding
streets had one. The idea was simple. A large sheet of
paper, preferably wallpaper, was pleated and then
pinned up to make a circle. A piece of wood then had
a split made at the top to hold the paper and, hey
presto, a desirable, designer paper umbrella.

We paraded around for hours but soon the wind
and rain made short work of them and the paper
parasols disappeared as fast as they had arrived.

Meanwhile, the boys had devised a far better toy.
After the start of the National Health Service, babies
were fed on National Dried Milk that came in tall
tins. Before long, some genius thought of punching
two holes in a tin and inserting long pieces of string.
This meant he or she could walk around as if on stilts,
albeit short stilts. Soon we were all asking mothers
with new babies to give us their old tins and it was
fortunate that there was a baby boom at the time,
which meant nearly every child had this wonderful
toy.

Another super game was 'Skiffies'. We would all
gather round a shop window and call out the initials
of some product on show. To the request of, 'Gie's a
skiffie,' the person who called out, put their hands

together and pointed in the general direction of the product.

If guessed, the chase round some convenient lamp-post was both noisy and annoying to the shop owner and our mums because often the chaser caught you by your clothes. It wasn't the first time someone went home with a hand-knitted jumper in holes and, in some cases, almost disintegrated with wool yarn hanging down in festoons.

Looking back, I can picture this scene as if it were yesterday. Long summer days in dusty streets with the shadows growing longer as night fell. Afterwards, with all the running and jumping and general mayhem, we would fall into bed and be fast asleep in moments, leaving behind the echo of our voices and pavements covered in chalk, hoping against hope that it wouldn't rain overnight and wash away all our carefully drawn games.

Last but not least, none of our playthings cost any money but believe me, they gave us hours and hours of fun and pleasure on the sunny streets of our childhood.

2

Verdant Works

In September 1996, Verdant Works in West Henderson's Wynd was opened to the public. Acquired in 1991 by Dundee Heritage Trust, they saved a vital part of Dundee's jute history and brought to life an important part of the city's involvement with the jute industry.

As I walked around the cavernous building I couldn't help but feel how quiet and empty it was and although it depicts an age gone by, nothing in my opinion can ever recreate the atmosphere of a jute mill in its heyday.

I imagined how bemused my mother and her pals would have been. A job, which to them was a daily grind of hard work in a stoury mill is now a tourist attraction.

What I remember most of all was the noise. Hundreds of looms clattering away as the weavers stood, hour after hour, with the shuttle, the weft and the warp of the hessian, coping with a pair of looms which needed total concentration. It was impossible to have a conversation with your neighbour because of this noise, and as a result this clamour led to a sign language being used that the workers were experts at.

Still, the weaver felt fortunate when the looms were working properly. Should the loom break down for some reason then it was the 'tenter' who had to sort out the problem. The tenter was a mechanic who fixed the looms, and weavers – who were on piece-work – were often at loggerheads with these men, especially if they didn't sort out the problem quickly, as it could lead to a few hours or worse, an entire morning or afternoon, when the weaver wasn't earning her wages.

Apart from the calender machines with their large steamrollers, which finished the cloth off to a smooth finish, the weaving sheds were at the final end of the process as rolls of hessian were disgorged from the looms.

However, long before the yarn was in the weaver's shuttle, the jute fibres the hessian had once been, had themselves been through lots of different processes.

When they arrived straight from the docks, the jute bales were taken to the batching and carding shed where they were sprayed with a mixture of oil and water to straighten and clean the fibres. During Dundee's whaling history it was whale oil that was used for the batching.

Another machine then discharged a continuous fibre called 'sliver'. This was then passed through another machine which made the strand even finer before the roving frames twisted the thread.

Then it was on to the spinning sheds that were also

noisy, dusty places. The roving machines holding hundreds of winding bobbins were manned by women who spent long hot days running up and down the aisles as each bobbin quickly filled with yarn.

The bobbins would then be wound onto 'cops' that would then be fitted into shuttles, which provided the weft thread for the weavers.

Working in the mills was a low paid job, although the weavers earned a bit more than the spinners, and there were no holidays with pay until well into the 1940s. This meant that families often went hungry until the next pay day after the annual summer break. I remember all too well this time of the year when money was tighter than ever.

We never had a holiday and it was such a worrying time for Mum, as we had to live for three weeks on one week's wages.

When paid holidays finally became law, I remember Mum going down to the mill near the end of the holiday period to collect her pay. What a relief it must have been to her.

Mill owners lived in large luxurious houses while their employees lived in damp, overcrowded, slum housing. Did they never give a thought to the workforce's terrible poverty and atrocious living conditions?

It seems not. Instead of providing better wages, the owners ploughed money into the railroads of America and the beef ranches of Argentina; buying shares in the wealth of other countries whilst ignoring the grinding poverty around them.

Oh, I know a lot of them were philanthropists, spending huge sums of money on various institutions in the city, like the Caird maternity wing and numerous other donations to the Dundee Royal Hospital, plus other many bequests like Baxter Park, the Caird Hall and Marryat Halls. And I dare say a hard-working city was grateful for their gifts.

However, these donations and gifts bypassed my mother and her pals, Nan, Bella and Nellie who all worked in the South Anchor jute mill in Anchor Lane, which was situated at the rear of the Verdant Works. Athough the demise of the jute industry lay many years into the future, the end did come eventually. The last cargo of jute arrived from India on board the ship *Banglar Urmi* in October 1998 and it heralded the end of an era.

Mum did enjoy her work because it brought great friends and a spirit of camaraderie to her life.

As I strolled around the Verdant Works sixty years later, was that cacophony of noise a far distant echo from the golden age of jute? Or was it the bemused mill workers laughing at the thought of their daily grind now being turned into a tourist attraction?

Now, of course, with the passage of time, it's fitting that part of our historic past is being preserved for future generations and it's right that young people can see for themselves the changes in work and conditions over the century, and can see how people, perhaps their ancestors, coped with hardship, poverty and the hard grinding work in the many jute mills of Dundee.

It is maybe wrong in the modern world to be aggrieved at the jute owners for their lack of concern for ordinary men and women who helped make their wealth. Still, I've often thought that these owners who lived in their palatial homes, their ivory towers, never knew that mill women such as Mum, Nan, Nellie or Bella ever existed.

But I'm afraid that was their loss.

The Weaver's Lament
The weaving looms clatter in a tumult of noise.
Strident, mechanical noises
That numb her brain and silence her tongue.
Questions are posed in sign language
As her neighbour asks the time.
Dear Lord it's only half past nine.
Here comes the gaffer, a thin joyless guy,
Stalking down the aisle
Like a grey thundercloud.
He's looking for skivers and broken-down looms,
His face etched with pain
From his varicose veins.
Only eight more hours till the end of the shift.
The looms will then shudder into a silence so complete
That the canopy of cobwebs
Stop quivering in the dusty corners.
This heavenly peace
Like a prisoner's release.

3

James 'Napper' Thomson

James 'Napper' Thomson was a native of Lochee and owner of a coach hire company and emporium. In 1945 he started his car and garage business in Kirk Street, a business that was to grow over the next few years. A shrewd businessman, he had many interests.

In our house, and like most of the population of Dundee, holidays in the 1960s were mostly always taken in this country. There was no fancy foreign travel or visits to exotic overseas locations.

Before the Dundee holiday fortnight, we would visit Napper Thomson's emporium in South Road, Lochee, and hire one of his caravanettes.

Packing four children, two adults, clothes and food into the caravanette took a lot of careful planning, which always went awry a couple of days into the holiday.

The caravanette wasn't a huge vehicle, but it was possible to stand upright because the roof had a wonderful striped contraption that lifted like an awning.

And so we would set off for glamorous locations

like Oban, Fort William or some other spot on the west coast.

As we bowled merrily along, it was with a feeling of freedom that we could stop anywhere on the road and cook a meal on the miniscule cooker.

If the weather was nice we could sit outside with our meal, but if it was raining, which it was more often than not, we all would crowd round the tiny table and try to dodge each other's elbows.

The sleeping arrangements were haphazard to say the least. As there didn't seem to be enough beds for everyone, I managed to squeeze in beside the children but my husband slept on the floor or stretched out on the front seats of the driving cab. That was until he discovered the pull-out hammock a couple of feet from the roof. Getting into it took all the patience of a contortionist but as we settled down for the night, he seemed as snug as the proverbial bug.

Now on this particular holiday, the weather was more like winter than summer and in the morning he was so cold that he nearly froze to the roof. That was the end of the hammock and it was back to the lottery of squeezing into a corner and trying to get a good night's sleep.

One holiday I'll never forget was in Oban. There had been a hurricane in the Caribbean and the west coast of Scotland got the tail end of it. I remember hanging a sheet out to air on a makeshift rope and it disappeared, sailing over Oban Bay like a sail without a ship. I almost cried because it was brand new and a bonny blue colour. The kids however, were ecstatic at the sight as it flapped like a gigantic bluebird towards the horizon.

The wind howled all night and the next morning we awoke to a scene of devastation, with overturned caravans littered all around us. Fortunately, it was a small privately-owned site and as all the caravans were empty, no one was hurt. For some unknown reason, we had stayed upright, probably due to the weight inside that had anchored the caravanette to the ground. Then we had the pleasure of the campsite toilet before leaving and had to wash in freezing cold water as the hot water system hadn't been switched on. The old man in charge of this small site was apologetic, but it didn't pay to switch on the hot water until the site was full, he said.

Although it has to be said that we were there in July, goodness only knows when the holiday season began. Perhaps there was a two-week window in August.

As I looked around the scene of devastation, I thought it highly unlikely that the site would ever open that year, and made a mental note to check out the washing arrangements before booking in anywhere else.

We made the decision to drive inland to escape the wind, stopping on a quiet road to make the breakfast. The kettle was almost boiling and the eggs were at the gooey stage in the frying pan when suddenly the Calor gas ran out. I couldn't believe it and tried to coax the eggs into something edible. However, all was in vain and I had to dump the half-cooked mess onto the roadside verge. And drinking lukewarm tea didn't help.

Still, we had this immediate crisis and what was the remedy? We were all hungry and I had a vision of my wee ones starving to death. We had to drive almost twenty miles before we found a small café that was open. The owners must have thought we were refugees from a biblical famine, as there wasn't as much as a crumb left on the tablecloth after we finished.

With no gas, we had to plan the next couple of days around cafés but we had loads of bread, butter and jam so we survived.

Taking the caravanette back after the holiday, Napper asked if we had enjoyed our holiday. When being told about the gas, he laughed and showed us a spare cylinder in a small cupboard. Talk about feeling stupid.

We had set off like pioneers in the great rural outdoors, but quite honestly the matriarchal head of the house was a 'townie' at heart.

At the time, I thought Napper just owned the garage, but I later discovered he also sold household items, carpets and linoleum.

Napper died on 25 February 1981 and his family carried on with the business.

As for me, well I will always remember him for his caravanettes with the telescopic striped roofs and the opportunity to sample the freedom of the roads.

It was perhaps just our bad luck that we hit the west coast in the wake of an American hurricane but it all added to the spirit of the holiday. Well, maybe it did afterwards. At the time, I didn't feel spirited and thought the entire week was one big chore.

One of Napper's other sidelines was buying up parachutes from surplus war stock. Perhaps a parachute would have made up for the missing sheet that by now was probably a blue floating blob in the mid-Atlantic? Or maybe it's reached the Bahamas?

4

Spookie Nights

Working in Wallace's busy restaurant in the 1950s was hectic from the minute it opened at 9 a.m. till closing time at 6.15 p.m.

Not only did it serve a busy lunch and high tea menu, but also had a steady stream of hungry customers who came in for bridies, pies and teas in the morning, or tea with bridies, pies and cakes in the afternoon.

The waitresses and kitchen workers were run off their feet except for a small breather when the lunchtime workers departed for their jobs.

This was the time when arrangements would be made for an exciting evening entertainment, namely the 'spookie nicht'. This was usually held in someone's house and, with a meal laid on, we would all gather on the tramcar and depart to whichever house was hosting the event.

The anticipation was intense but someone, usually Nan, always warned us to, 'mak shair you dinnie gie oot ony information aboot yersel.'

Seemingly, the fortune-teller picked up 'vibrations' when listening to chatter at the tea table and was then able to 'tell yer fortune.'

Because the fortune-teller was also having her tea with us I always thought it made for a strained atmosphere and, speaking personally, I was afraid to open my mouth, which must have been a first in my life.

As we scoffed our bacon and eggs or cold ham salad, I would sit in silence, only nodding or shaking my head when spoken to, and the poor fortune wifie must have thought I was deaf and dumb and daft. But I wasn't letting any secrets out. After all, she was getting paid to tell me all about my life, wasn't she?

Sometimes we would all sit in a circle and get 'oor fortunes telt' en masse. This was fine because nothing of any interest ever came out. Oh, we were told the usual spiel about handsome men and money coming to us, and trips over water. Well, this was nothing new as most of us had a man in our lives, albeit some more handsome than others, money was always being passed over in the shape of customers' tips and didn't we all travel frequently over on the 'Fifie', the ferry that took passengers and vehicles from Craig Pier to Newport in Fife?

Sometimes we would get our teacups read. The woman would sit with the cup in her hands like it was the holy grail and turn it around while peering into the mass of dark tea leaves.

Turning the cup upside down, when some drips of tea spilled onto the saucer she would utter in a doom-laden, solemn voice, 'Ye'll be shedding tears afore lang.' But then on a cheerier note, she would suddenly see a long trip filled with wonder: 'Yer ga'en on a journey ower watter but thir's joy and money at the end of it.' And there was always a ring in all our cups. 'Thir's a marriage coming.' Or if it wasn't a marriage then it would be a christening, lots of money or letters coming 'ower the sea.'

Oh the pleasure of knowing how happy we were all going to be with such a fortune.

Being young and daft I always longed to hear something scandalous or juicy about a co-worker but like ectoplasm, it never materialised. That is until one night when, quite honestly, we were all becoming a bit jaded by the usual 'handsome man' etc.

I remember the night vividly. It was a cold winter's night and we were all freezing as we hurried into the house. The first surprise was it wasn't the usual 'wifie' but a man and he, seemingly, was a well-known clairvoyant. 'He kens a' aboot yer life so dinnie hide onything,' said the hostess.

Well that was fine by me because it meant I could chatter as I ate my tea. Another surprise was the fact he wanted to see everyone in private. A small bedroom was placed at his disposal and a small fire had even been lit in the tiny fireplace.

I think I was about the middle of the hierarchy to go into the room and I had had plenty of time to listen to the stories as, one by one, the other women emerged. They all spoke in whispers about their consultation and the general consensus was, 'That man's braw. He telt me things naebody else kens.'

Well, by the time it was my turn, the hair was standing up on the back of my neck and I was filled

17

with a mixture of anticipation, fear and horror; not quite the normal feelings at these events. I popped my head around the door and he fixed his eyes on me. I almost ran out the room when he said he felt a bolt of excitement on seeing me. However, he was only talking about my aura. I wondered if I'd let anything slip at the tea table but as I had never heard of anyone's aura, I knew I hadn't. I won't go into detail about the reading except to say a lot of it came true.

Afterwards, we all gathered at the tram stop as we discussed our fortunes. Quite a few of us were shivering but whether because of the readings or the cold night, I don't know.

Later, most of us said that fortune-telling was just a bit of fun; a nice tea, a wee wifie chattering on and finally a song from Emily, a woman who worked in the kitchen who had the most marvellous singing voice.

Yes, going to a 'spookie nicht' brought a frisson of pleasure, anticipation and fun into our lives whilst waiting for a good-looking man, money and travel over water. And if it meant playing daft to a wee wifie who picked up vibrations at the table then so be it.

Later, it was back to the mundane job of serving bridies, pies and cakes, soup and steak pie, and egg and chips with tea and toast.

Looking back, was it all mumbo jumbo? Well maybe.

And another thought. Do I still have the exciting aura or has it diminished over the years? I'll have to consult the crystal ball.

5

The City Arcade

Before the age of the supermarkets and big multinational stores, Dundee was a city of small, privately-owned little shops. Places like the Hub in the High Street; a miniscule newsagent's shop that was the width of a doorway and squashed in between H. Samuel's jewellery shop and the Maypole Grocery Store.

The Overgate also had a plethora of tiny shops, some of them below street level like the Auld Dundee Rock Shop, and it was the same in most streets with a corner shop that was the hub of the area.

During my childhood, my favourite place was the City Arcade, situated behind the massive bulk of the Caird Hall. It was ahead of its time in the fact that it was a forerunner of the shopping mall. With its two entrances on Shore Terrace, the arcade had a large selection of shops and was a Mecca for the citizens of the town.

It was possible to buy most things here; shops ranged from Imrie's Flowers to Mitchell's Poultry, from Cantrell's Fish to Frank Russell's Books, not forgetting the butcher and draper's shops, the linoleum merchant, The Radiant Health Centre and Puckel's Fancy Goods. It was like entering a vault with shops on either side. Small businesses adjoining each other had the aroma of cooked chickens and fresh flowers vying for attention.

There was the children's amusement centre with its collection of slot machines and this corner was always abuzz on Saturdays as hordes of children regularly descended with their pocket money, my brother and I included.

At the far end of the arcade, where a tunnel led up to the stairs that took you onto the City Square, was another selection of slot and game machines. This was a place of echoes, ghostly footsteps and distorted voices. There was always a sinister air here, but this was probably due to its isolation from the friendly shops and also the fact that cold winds regularly whistled down the stairs and along the tunnel.

In the Arcade, my favourite shop was Puckel's. He sold just about everything under the sun, or so it seemed at the time. All I can remember was the window filled with scores of bangles, pairs of earrings, necklaces and ornaments.

If you wanted to buy anything you usually stood at this window and Mr Puckel would accompany you as you pointed out the item. Then it was a simple operation for him to retrieve it and a sale was made. The funny thing was, the window never had any spaces, no matter how many customers there were.

My mother bought her linoleum from Joseph

Miller. His shop wasn't large enough to hold all his stock, hence the rows and rows of patterned linoleum standing to attention outside the shop like sentinels guarding a fortress.

I think there was a chain or rope around these rolls of lino, which in today's markets wouldn't be out of place. Away back then, when health and safety didn't amount to much, it was a forerunner of things to come.

Still, the owner was only being careful of his stock because of the passing trade, the scores of potential customers touching the lino and milling around, not to mention all the noisy children running about in different directions. I often wondered what would happen if these rolls did tumble over. Would they roll out into Shore Terrace, knocking people over like skittles, then swerve into the Corporation buses as they waited at their stances?

Sadly, I never did find out.

My mother's purchase was a congoleum square. This was a cheaper version of linoleum and was usually brightly patterned. Also, being a square meant that, when laid, the edges of the floorboards were on show.

A tin of varnish darkened the floorboards but it was a devil to keep the floor clean. Dust always seemed to gather in fluffy balls and one day my brother wrote his name in the stour, much to my annoyance.

It was my job to go around with a duster and clean up the dust but I had better things to do that week. Namely to get engrossed in my new library book, which meant I completely forgot the floor chore.

Later on, the arcade continued to survive with different shops and I have been told that there was a coin-operated figure of Trigger, the horse ridden by Roy Rogers in all his cowboy pictures. Although Roy Rogers belonged to a different generation, children seemingly had great pleasure sitting on Trigger. Roy Rogers and Trigger were great favourites of the Picture House and when they came to Britain he was mobbed by adults and children alike. I've also been told that this same coin-operated figure has been on sale on eBay, advertised as broken and needing attention and some tender, loving care. Considering what an icon it was, it deserves nothing less.

Unlike the broken Trigger, the arcade needed more than attention and TLC and it was demolished to make way for the towering Tayside House.

Shore Terrace is now a quiet place. The bus stances have long gone, along with the Arcade. No longer do families and hordes of children come to shop or catch a bus. Tayside House now sits in silence at weekends. Not like the Saturdays of old when the place was alive with the smell of diesel and children's laughter, cooked chickens and fragrant flowers.

As for the stark symmetry of Tayside House? Will writers be reminiscing over this building in the future? Will it be held with the same affection as the old City Arcade?

Maybe. But not, I think, by the hundreds of customers who passed through its doors over the years.

6

The City Centre Bar

My cousin's father-in-law owned the City Centre Bar, which stood on the corner of Shore Terrace and Dock Street. It was a very busy bar and, along with regular customers who were quite happy to stand or sit with their pints of beer, the bar was also visited by a wonderful group of 'worthies'.

One customer offered to somersault over a line of chairs in exchange for a pint and he was successful. However, on the offer of another pint to do the trick again, he landed on his head.

There was much consternation but the man picked himself up, shook his head and downed his drink. He must have had a very thick skull. Still, he went away, obviously none the worse for his high jinks.

Another guy would regularly do handstands and on one occasion, two men offered him a free pint if he would do a handstand out on the pavement for twenty minutes.

Now the pub had two doors and whilst the man was faithfully standing on his hands, the two customers left by the other door. After an hour, the barman had to go outside to tell him there was going to be no free beer. He was furious. But quite honestly, I would also have been annoyed. After all a bet is a bet.

One night, just before Christmas, a man came in with two dogs on leads. He had a long coat on with lots of pockets and there were puppies in some of the pockets plus one down the front of his coat. He was a walking dog kennel.

Suddenly a tray was banged down on the bar counter and all the dogs took fright, running off in all directions with the man chasing them onto the street. One or two of the puppies hid under the tables and were purloined by customers.

'This'll mak a braw present for the bairn's Christmas,' said one man, tucking the puppy down the front of his coat and hurrying off. Meanwhile, the poor original dog owner was probably scouring the entire length of Dock Street for his missing canines.

Whether he ever found them all is a mystery.

Mr McRobbie's son Alistair also owned a dog called Mac who was often in the bar. One day, a customer drew the shape of a bone on the floor and told Mac to guard it. Another customer laughed and told the first man not to be so daft.

'Dae ye think the dog will be sae daft as tae no ken it's a chalk mark?'

When the artist went to the toilet, the man decided to test out his theory of stupidity. Mac however growled so loudly whilst guarding his chalky bone that the customer left with a very white face.

Mac was a character. He would regularly run off home to Craigiebarns or, if he was feeling tired, hop on the bus. One day a bus conductor came into the bar to complain that the dog was standing at the top of the stairs of the double-decker bus and wouldn't let anyone past.

Exit one disgruntled dog and a bar full of amused customers.

Blind Mattie would also come in on a regular basis, wearing her Salvation Army poke bonnet and selling *The War Cry*.

Blind Mattie was a weel kent figure around Dundee. Born Martha Wallace in Main Street in 1875, she would go round the streets playing her melodeon and singing. One of her favourite songs was 'My Ain Folk'. With her faithful companion Maggie Nicol who had been with her since they were both young, they managed to make a living for years before ill health and old age meant both going to live in Rowans Eventide Home. Before she died in 1962, Mattie had a standing ovation at the Johnny Victory Charity Concert that was held in the Caird Hall.

Maggie had been hired by Mattie's father to look after his daughter and it was a splendid example of friendship that kept the two women together for all their lives. Maggie also died at The Rowans.

One Saturday, a football team from the west coast was playing in the city. In those days the bars closed at 9.30 p.m. but it was impossible to get the supporters out of the bar. It was bedlam with men stamping and singing and waving banners.

They were also lighting small pieces of paper and

dropping them on the floor so it would seem that the football hooligan isn't a new thing. It was midnight before the owner got the door closed and even then the men continued to hammer at the doors. Bottles and glasses were jumping around on the shelves and Eleanor, my cousin, recalls it was a hard job to keep everything from tumbling down and breaking. Still, the City Centre Bar wasn't alone with all this trouble as most of the central bars also had their share of noisy customers. It was a relief when the supporters were all safely on their buses and heading home.

It must have been an exciting bar with wonderful customers, with quite a few of them making a lasting impression.

Do pubs today have such entertaining customers on their premises like somersaulting acrobats and drinkers who stand on their hands? Or a walking dog kennel and chalky bones on the floor? I don't think so.

Now, a giant television screen seems to dominate some pubs with the clientele all watching some programme or other. If Mac the dog even ventured the slightest growl he would be evicted or, worse, totally ignored.

Sadly, the pub is no longer there. Like its eccentric clientele it is all now history, which is a great pity.

7

Radio Days

Listening to the wireless was a great pleasure for thousands of people in the days before television, especially on cold winter nights, sitting around the fire being entertained by a whole variety of programmes.

Some people listened to the Home Service, which we thought was a bit highbrow. We much preferred The Light Programme.

Mum loved the comedy shows like *Round the Horne*, *Ray's a Laugh*, *The Clitheroe Kid* and *Take it from Here* with Jimmy Edwards and *The Glums*, a family with the most monotonous voices. Mum also liked a comedian called Reg Dixon who signed off his programme with a song called 'Confidentially'.

George and I adored *Dick Barton Special Agent* with its creepy 'Devil's Gallop' theme tune. It always ended on a cliffhanger when the announcer would come in with a preview of the next night's listening with the chilling words: 'Will Dick, Jock and Snowy escape, and will Kate be rescued from the burning barn?' At this point I was almost falling off my seat in fear.

On Sundays, we always listened to *Two-Way Family Favourites* with Jean Metcalfe in Britain and Cliff Mitchelmore in Germany, which played records for families separated by National Service. Young lads sending messages of undying love to their girlfriends and the girls sending back hopes of an early reunion in order to get married.

'This is a message from Bert in BFPO wherever to Gladys. He's sending all his love and can't wait till he gets home in ten months time.' Then Jeannie would send her love to Norrie in BFPO somewhere: 'Can't wait till our wedding next year. I've got the dress and everything's organised and I'm counting the days.'

Oh the romance of it all. I almost swooned at some of the messages.

Mum however was the usual unromantic cynic. 'Eh jist hope she's no left wi' the frock and the cake. Thir's mony a slip atween the cup and the lip is aw eh can say.'

I decided to ignore her and listen to the next heartfelt plea from across the sea.

The one programme we disliked was *Sing Something Simple*. There didn't seem to be any highs and lows in the singing, or any passion. But that was just our opinion.

Another pleasure was going to the pictures. Dundee was well provided with picture houses. I read somewhere that there were twenty-eight in total and I quite believe it.

We had our own little circle that we used regularly: The Plaza in The Hilltown, the Empire in Rosebank Road and the Tivoli in Bonnybank Road.

The Empire had terrible toilets. The wall between the ladies and gents had a huge hole at floor level. How anyone had managed to make a hole this size was a mystery. How did the wall chiseller have time to make such a huge hole? And did no one ever notice him (or her)?

I was always frightened when using them. Mum would come with me and stand guard outside the door, just in case a huge hairy arm grabbed my legs. But in all the years we went to the Empire, nothing ever happened. I guess the hole remained until the building was demolished. Very mysterious.

Mum could only afford the cheap seats which meant, if you were unlucky, you could be sitting in the front row, almost eyeball to eyeball with the film stars and craning your neck in the bargain.

Forever the strategist, Mum had a ploy. The ninepenny seats and the one and thruppenny seats were separated by a thick red cord. If you were quick you could bag two seats right beside this cord and imagine yourself in the luxury of the dearer seats.

Once Mum bought the tickets, I would run ahead like a sprinter and grab two seats. For some reason lost in the mists of time, George never accompanied us. Five minutes later she would come plodding up the aisle while I gaily waved to make sure she saw me.

I loved Betty Grable and all the glamorous Hollywood musicals. Another favourite was Doris Day and my one abiding memory of her is starring in

Romance on the High Seas. Dressed in a lovely shimmering dress, she sang the wonderful song 'It's Magic'. She wasn't the only one to think it was magic because I was entranced and since then I've been a lifelong fan.

Mum, on the other hand, adored Alastair Sim. I always thought him a bit creepy but that was probably the roles he played in his films.

Betty Grable reputedly had legs insured for a million dollars and they were always on show in the films. I expect the film studio wanted to make money from such a fabulous film star. I used to look at my legs and dream of being another Betty Grable while Mum would shake her head at me.

At the time, I thought everyone in America lived like the film stars, in fabulous houses and with wonderful clothes and food, which, incidentally, no one ever ate. To the wartime masses who had to cope with rationing, this was awful and I used to try and identify every dish on the table, leaving the cinema with my stomach rumbling.

With hindsight it was all a sham. Oh, the stars may have had money and fame but they all had their problems like us lesser mortals. But at the time I was swept away with the sheer glamour of it all.

The picture houses didn't open on a Sunday so it was back to the wireless. My teenage years were spent listening to Radio Luxembourg.

My favourite programme was the *Top Twenty Hit Parade*, sponsored by Sta-blonde and Brunette shampoos, and some guy who had a sure fire way to make money with his foolproof football forecast.

However, always keen to have an evening with fear, Mum and I often listened to *The Black Museum* with Valentine Dyall, a man with a sonorous voice who gave us shivers just listening to him.

One very dark winter's night, we were listening intently to some blood-curdling tale when Mum decided to put the kettle on. On reaching the lobby, she saw a hand coming through the letter box. Running into the living room, she started pushing me towards the window.

'Quick, get oot the windae and run for the bobby. Thir's a maniac trying tae get intae the hoose.'

Of course by this time I was as panic-stricken as she was and the window was now wide open. Pushing me out, she said, 'Run and get the bobby.'

I tried to reason with her, mainly because I wasn't a hundred per cent sure the maniac wasn't waiting to grab me when I was outside, but she just pushed me further out into the darkness.

Thankfully, we lived on the ground floor otherwise I would have been a fatality in the next day's news paper. As I crept out through the gate, I saw a figure coming towards me. I almost fainted until I realised it was my brother.

'Eh'm trying tae get the key,' he said.

Our door key was tied to a bit of string and hung behind the letter box, but for some reason it had been moved up beside the lock.

The funny thing was, instead of hammering on the door like George, I climbed back in through the window like an idiot.

My mother's face was a picture when she saw

George. 'Och eh thocht it wis you aw the time,' she said.

I thought, oh no you didn't. But then neither did I.

It was more thrilling to think a maniac was on the loose.

My brother looking for the key was most definitely an anti-climax.

8

David Phillips

I never met David Phillips but I could honestly swear I knew him. For years I had read his pawkie stories about Dundee; stories about street life and ordinary people he met on his travels throughout his life and all told in the Dundee dialect, or 'Dundonese' as someone once said. In fact, I would say that reading Davie's articles and books gave me the impetus to start my own writing career.

He was a modest man with simple needs, a painter and decorator before he took up writing, but it is through his writing that we remember the man.

How well I remember laughing out loud at his exploits in his books, *Eh Never Fell Intae a Midden*, *The Lichty Nichts* and *Meh Dundee*, also identifying with the gossiping wifies and wee working men and other assorted characters that he regularly put down in print.

He was born in Lochee in St Mary Street and although he loved the bustle of the busy streets, he also loved going off to the hills with his camera, as photography was another one of his talents.

Just after the war, he went off to Grimsby with another painter/decorator, to start up their own business, but after a while he came back to Lochee because his mother wasn't in the best of health.

He lived in Quarryside for many many years and was a huge help to his neighbours and others who lived beside him.

Every morning he would regularly go around the neighbours' doors and offer to get their messages and newspapers for them.

This quiet, unassuming man who believed in caring for others, never married, but he was passionate in the good old-fashioned belief of good neighbourliness, kindness and modesty.

He was once asked what he thought was the greatest invention and he laughed when he answered 'The plastic bag.' I believe he was never without a plastic bag on his trips to the shops.

Sadly, Davie died very suddenly on 13 January 1987 in the sub post office in Lochee, a very sad day for everyone who knew him; from the people, who lived beside him, editors and staff of the newspapers that published his stories, Jimmy Shand whose biography he wrote, and Douglas Phillips, the artist who had planned with Davie, an exhibition of paintings and photos.

And why did I get the feeling I knew him although we had never met? Well back in the days after the war when he went to Grimsby with a painter colleague, that friend was my Father. I only learned this fact a year or so ago from my Uncle Jack.

I remember the time so vividly when my father was

planning on leaving for Grimsby, all the uncertainty in the family and my mother fearful of the hardship it would cost. Davie must have been around us at the time, but there were so many people around in those days that this quiet, modest and very clever man must have slipped under my radar and that truly, for me, is the saddest part of all.

His obituary said he wanted to be 'a bother tae naebody.' And he never was.

9

Street Entertainment

Perhaps it was because people lived in small, cramped tenement houses that nearly everyone congregated onto the streets for entertainment, from meeting friends and getting a good daily dose of fresh air.

Mind you, a lot of the air in the city wasn't that fresh with all the smoking chimneys belching out thick, black smoke. It was, however, a better bet than sitting in the equally smoky and poky rooms that were the working population's lot.

There was a variety of things do at street level. Sundays in particular were boring with the picture houses and dance halls closed, not to mention the pubs for the older generation, although a lot of people got around this by travelling the required three miles to some hotel as a 'bona fide' traveller.

It was the law that this 'traveller' had to sign a book, stating where he or she was travelling to and the licensing body must have noted how many travellers decided to visit different places within a three-mile radius of Dundee every Sunday.

On a healthier note was the Dundee Thistle

Cycling Club, that had its meeting point in Milton Street. Every weekend the cyclists would gather for their weekly run. My husband had a pal who was a member and when asked where the particular trip had been, he always replied, 'the Sma Glen.' The glen between Aberfeldy and Crieff.

This wasn't entirely true because the club regularly went far afield and often stayed in the Youth Hostels before cycling back on the Sunday with huge bunches of heather tied onto their handlebars.

Willie Keir, who had a baker's shop in Kirkton where my husband was an apprentice baker, was also a staunch member.

Ally recalls getting a loan of a bike from him during the Dundee holiday fortnight and was told to cycle to Skye before perhaps considering whether to join the club. Ally however preferred to cycle alone and regularly went miles at the weekend to Callander, St Fillans and Crieff.

On this particular holiday, he went to Comrie and stayed with his two uncles, cycling every day. At the end of the holiday he left Comrie later than planned, but he had to get back home to start work the following morning. It was a nasty wet day and he got soaked on the journey back. It was also dark by the time he reached his road end and his mum and dad were standing outside the close, worried about him.

The next day when Ally told his boss he didn't get to Skye, Willie took the bike back. Perhaps if he had stopped to count up the cycling miles actually done over the two weeks they would have amounted to going to John O' Groats and back. But Willie didn't do that and his behaviour was churlish to say the least.

Running was another pastime and the Hawkhill Harriers and Dundee Road Runners' Club catered for runners of all ages, regularly staging events or having their members winning races in other parts of the country.

On 24 April 1983, the City of Dundee People's Marathon attracted 1,343 entrants. That very first marathon was a great success with hundreds of people turning out to witness the event. Don McGregor from St Andrews was the winner.

The 1986 race saw Colin Youngson in first place with runners M. McNaught, Sam Graves and C. Ross in the next three places, while my son George Reynolds was seventh. The first woman home was Morag McTaggart.

In 1987, Terry Mitchell won the hard slog of twenty-six miles with Charlie Hasket, Sam Graves and George taking the next three places. The first woman home was J. Danskin. Sam Graves went on to win the 1988 race but by then the half marathon and 10k races were becoming more popular, and this was followed by the Hawkhill Harriers Centenary 10k race on 23 April 1989, which attracted hundreds of participants, including children.

On this occasion George came second and on 14 May in the City of Dundee People's 10km race, George finished fifth with Peter McColgan coming in first and his Olympic-winning wife, Liz finishing in eighth position.

1989 also saw the Hawkhill Harriers centenary

dinner on 15 September at the Earl Gray Hotel. The late, great and very funny writer and comedian George Duffus, who had been a member of the Harriers in his younger days, was the speaker.

My son ran other marathons and finished first at Humber, Wick and Loch Rannoch but he also entered the Miami and New York marathons and other races worldwide. However, like other athletes, he preferred the shorter races.

Sadly, the numbers declined for the full marathon and the last one was run in 1991, but anyone who witnessed these running years will remember the carnival spirit, not to mention the money raised for charities.

The Dundee Road Runners still have races. On a beautiful day last autumn when the trees were a delight of gold and russet colours, my oldest son Alick ran in a 10k race from Templeton Woods to the finishing line above the old Timex factory.

As for myself, well I've never been athletic and my only brush with walking for miles was the 'Monkey Parade' in the 1950s. On Sundays, crowds of young people would gather and parade up and down the Overgate, hoping no doubt to catch the eye of some girl or boy.

With my four dancing pals, Violet, Zena, Mima and Margaret, I would walk up and down for hours, chattering and having a jolly good time. I can't recall if they caught any boy's eye. I know I didn't.

What I recall best from these outings was my green coat. Mum had let me choose, for the first time, my own coat. And what a coat it turned out to be. I bought it from Grafton's Fashion Shop in the Murraygate. It was green and almost fluorescent.

Mum said, 'If thir's oany fowk on the moon, they'll see ye for hundreds o' miles.' Still I loved it and the only regret I have is that it had gone to the great textile heaven when American astronaut Neil Armstrong landed on the moon.

I remembered Mum's words and I wonder if he would have loved my coat as much as I did back in the days of the 'Monkey Parade'.

Also parading the streets during the 'Monkey Parade' were a couple of big, burly policemen who kept ushering us onto the pavements. 'Move alang now, keep aff the road,' they said, as we all crowded around the narrow pavements. Although I didn't know it then, one of these policemen was to be my future father-in-law.

At the time I was always in awe of these big guys as they looked like they took no nonsense from anyone. Later, after I got to know him, I realised he was a great practical joker in his day and he was always full of stories from his days on the beat.

My husband recalls having to go to a cobbler's shop in the Hawkhill to pick up his working boots and he had to take a pal with him so they could carry one boot each. They were a size fourteen. As my mother would have said at the time, 'He had a guid grip o Scotland.'

Finally, although never an entrant in the city's marathons, my husband had the pleasure of a 'Pram Push'. Before he started his apprenticeship in 1952, he worked for a year as a lift boy in Smith Brothers, one of the large department stores in the city – D.M. Browns and G.L. Wilson being the other two.

One day, the manager asked him to push a large Silver Cross pram to an address in Glamis Road. On reaching the house, the elderly woman was astounded at a pram arriving at her door. 'Thir's nae bairns here,' she said.

A bit of head scratching ensued till they came up with the answer. The pram was meant to go to Old Glamis Road, which lay miles in the opposite direction. Finally arriving at the destination, the pram was duly handed over. We often wondered if this was the only 'Pram Push' marathon in Dundee and did the pram wheels need a retread?

Oh those happy, innocent times.

Shall we ever see their return?

10

Travelling the Roads to Dundee

Over the centuries, Dundee has always been a town to which immigrants flocked. My own ancestors came from Ireland in the 1800s to work in the jute mills, as did thousands of other Irish people. They settled mostly in Lochee, probably because of Cox's jute mill complex.

Even the names of streets reflected this mass movement of people. Places like Atholl Street, which was called 'Tipperary' and another area called 'The Bog'. They brought with them the customs of the Emerald Isle and although the majority of families lived in desperate conditions and were forever on the edge of poverty, their traditions are still alive in many communities to this day.

Such was the influx that it was noted in 1830 that there was one Catholic priest for 2,000 Irish people, but ten years later that figure had risen to 7,100 and almost all were working in thè linen and flax works. By 1861, the rise in immigration reached 14,366, nearly fifteen per cent of the population, mainly all working in the jute mills.

Without the skill of these workers, it is doubtful if the jute mills could have coped with the huge demand for their products.

Another group of immigrants were the Italian families who were also a huge asset to the city. They set up wonderful ice cream shops and the tasty 'chippers'; fish and chip businesses which fed a great deal of the population and still do.

They had super exotic names as well. Names like Dellanzo, Soave, Zanre and Fugaccia. Our local chip shop was Dellanzo's on the Hilltown and their fish, pudding and pie suppers filled many a hungry stomach during the dark wartime rationing.

I recall after the war when the elderly parents of the Dellanzo family opened their small ice cream shop next to the chip shop. They seemed to appear from nowhere but I think they must have suffered the indignities of internment after Italy entered the war. It would seem that no matter how long they had lived in the country, they were looked on as a threat to national security. Thankfully, they stayed and prospered.

During the war, ice cream, wafers and cones were in short supply and my husband recalls being served ice cream on a sheet of paper from Nolli's shop in Strathmore Avenue.

There was also a big mirror behind the counter and on being asked if the shop had any sweets or cigarettes, Mr Nolli would be very apologetic and shake his head. What he didn't know was that the boxes stashed under the counter were visible in the mirror.

Still most shops were the same. They kept the

stock for their good customers. I worked for a short time at Primo and Lena Zaccarini's chip shop in Dudhope Street. It wasn't a large shop but it did have a seating area at the back and boy was it busy.

I started at four o'clock on a Saturday night and it was a constant slog of wrapping up cod or haddock suppers. I think they cost one and ninepence each, with the haddock being a few pennies dearer. Then there was the running about serving the seated customers.

I had an hour's break from seven o'clock and, as I jumped on a tramcar, I remember the chip and vinegar aroma that clung to my clothes and within minutes the smell would be all over the tram.

Then it was back to work until midnight with huge queues forming out into the street. I often thought the entire population bought chips on a Saturday. Even the policemen, who regularly patrolled the area from the police box at the foot of the Hilltown, came in for their suppers.

There was one customer who came in during my time with the shop. I remember she was at school with me but her family had emigrated to Canada. They must have come back for a holiday because she came into the shop with this strange accent. It was neither Dundee dialect nor English. Privately I called it 'Canadese'.

Primo asked her about her new home and she gossiped on about how different words were used in Canada. 'Chips are called French fries over there,' she said, in Canadese.

I know the term 'French fries' is used all the time

now but it was the first time I had heard the words. I couldn't understand it and was quite indignant. 'Why are they no called Italian fries?' I asked.

Some years later, people arrived from Pakistan, India and China and more layers were added to the tapestry of the city. Many of the Asian community now own small shops and they work long hours and give great service to customers. You only have to look around the streets to see the Indian and Chinese restaurants serving curries and naan bread, spring rolls and fried rice, plus lots more delicious dishes; food that would have been totally exotic, exciting and unknown fifty years ago.

Meanwhile, the good old fish and chips still reigns supreme, as do the ice cream sliders and cones, but we now have the pizza parlours, which add another addition to people's diets.

Nowadays, the city has seen a boom in people from Poland and other Eastern European countries and the University also brings in students from around the world, turning Dundee into a multicultural city.

Yes, we have a lot to be thankful for, that all these people from different countries decided to travel the roads to Dundee, staying and bringing up their families and bringing new ideas and talents into the melting pot of the city.

11

Piggyback Flying

In the autumn of 1938, a flying event took place that has never again been attempted. My grandad stood along with thousands of people at the King George V dock in Dundee to witness this event.

According to the story told to me years later, I should have been with him but, at two months old, my mother wasn't keen for him to carry me in my shawl and stand around along with hordes of spectators.

Not that it matters because I wouldn't have known a thing about this world attempt but by all accounts it was a wonderful sight, this 'piggyback flight'.

It was the time of the Munich Crisis and superiority in the air was gaining ground. Also, there was the difficulty of delivering mail to the far-flung countries of the British Empire.

One solution to the flat-rate Empire air mile service were the piggyback planes, *The Mercury* and *The Maia*, which consisted of the main seaplane, *The Maia*, with the smaller flying boat, *The Mercury*, on its back.

Maia was to take off and at a certain height, which I believe was 11,000 feet, *Mercury* would then disengage and fly towards her destination.

Although Short brothers built the plane in the south of England, Dundee was chosen for this thrilling flight, not because James Chalmers had introduced the first postage stamp, but because of the long distance record. It was to fly non-stop to Cape Town.

It was becoming an increasingly uneasy world with Hitler's Nazi Party in power in Germany and the Germans were already trying to fly planes from the decks of ocean liners. The Soviets had also completed a flight over the North Pole, a journey of 6,306 miles. The Air Ministry, determined not to be left behind, backed the scheme and the two planes landed in Dundee on September 1938 where they were berthed at the Catalina Flying Boat Station in Woodhaven.

It was to be the start of delays and bad luck due to the weather and technical problems. However, on 6 October with an Australian pilot called Captain Bennett at the controls and his co-pilot and radio operator First Officer Ian Harvey, *Maia* with her piggyback companion *Mercury* sped across the waves of the River Tay and slowly rose into the air. Then, in the skies over Angus, *Mercury* took off alone for South Africa.

Bad luck stayed with the two pilots as they flew over France, North Africa and the Sahara Desert. Ice on the wings over the South of England forced the plane to drop height, an engine cowling panel was lost and a combination of severe weather and strong head winds all contributed to the flight running out of fuel.

Before this, however, the two pilots had the scary experience of having to crawl out onto the fuselage to pump the fuel by hand.

The plane eventually landed on the Orange River, which was 350 miles short of Cape Town and sadly, a mere 260 miles short of the Soviet airmen's achievement.

The Mercury had however broken the German record of 5,215 miles by flying 6,045 miles in forty-two hours. It was a wonderful flight by the two pilots and the gutsy seaplane and this record has never been beaten.

What a great day it must have been for the plane's creator Robert Mayo, who was an aeronautical expert with Imperial Airlines. His dream of launching a piggyback plane had proved successful, but whether it ever became a viable commercial success, I don't know.

What I do know is that history was made on that cool October day in 1938 on the River Tay, and the thousands of spectators who saw it must have gone home with this knowledge. I know my grandad did.

12

A Ghost Story

During the autumn and winter when the evenings
were dark, a few of us girls would gather in someone's
close and tell stories. Sitting on the cold steps I could
feel the dampness seeping through my frock and in
this ideal setting with the feeble gas lamp casting
long, flickering shadows, I would tell my ghost
stories. Each story got more bizarre, but I had a
captive audience who would visibly shiver and keep
turning around as if some spook was coming behind
them.

Later, when it was time to leave, we would all be
scared out of our wits and all running for the safety of
our houses.

One day, one of the mothers complained to my
mum about me scaring her daughter. 'Meh lassie wis
that feared when she came hame. Said the ghost was
efter her.'

I got a stiff telling-off but as the girls always
demanded another ghost story, who was I not to
oblige? But comeuppance comes to us all.

After one deliciously gruesome story, I set off for my close. As was my normal practice, I would call up to mum and she would open the door, letting the light spill down the stairs. I was on the point of calling up to get mum to open the door when an apparition loomed out of the darkness.

My screams must have been heard in Fife and I took off down the Hilltown with the ghost and its companion chasing me. I was almost at Victoria Road when they caught me.

It turned out to be a young courting couple who had been standing in the darkness of my close saying goodnight to one another. The girl was wearing a white chiffon scarf around her hair and it was this luminous object that had given me such a fright.

Of course, the couple were apologetic and escorted me home where my very irate mother was waiting. In fact, she wasn't so much irate as blinking well furious.

'Eh'm sorry we gave the wee lassie a fricht,' said the young man, handing my mother a thruppenny bit. 'This'll buy her a sweetie.'

Of course my mum refused the money. 'Gie her a sweetie, eh'll gie her mair than that for waking up half the street, the wee toerag.'

Then the couple went on their way, a romantic long goodbye spoiled by a toerag. Well my mother went on and on, even when we were in bed.

The next morning, along came one of our neighbours. 'Eh've telt that lassie o' yours no tae tell her damn ghost stories. Meh lassie never slept last nicht. She kept saying there wis a ghost in the room.'

Mum said she understood and said, 'Eh think ye'll

find thit there will be nae mair stories. It wisnae jist your lassie thit got a fricht eh can tell ye.'

And she was right. My brush with the ghost lady with the chiffon scarf certainly put me off ghosts for a long time.

Well, maybe for a month or two.

13

Making a Living

Long before the advent of the Welfare State and National Health Service in 1948, trying to make a living could be very difficult, more so in times of recession and unemployment.

Dundee had its share of street hawkers and itinerate folk all trying to 'mak a bob or twa' – or in most cases 'a maik or a penny' – and what wonderful characters they were, trying to survive with only the basics in living accommodation and wares to sell.

One of these street hawkers was 'Pie Jock' who died in 1863. During his life he sold pans and jugs but was also a purveyor of hot pies. In these days of health and safety, it is inconceivable that he carried a hot oven fired by coal on his shoulder.

A Mr Peebles who had a shop in Perth Road made the pies and Jock would carry his oven around, calling out 'hot pehs, only tuppence each.'

He managed to eke out a living until pies became available in some shops and the bottom fell out of the portable hot pie business. Mr Peebles stopped selling pies to his wandering vendor and poor Jock was left to try and earn another living by selling small items.

Jock was described as being short and bent to one side. No doubt by having to carry a hot oven day in and day out. It's a wonder he wasn't scorched, or worse, badly burned.

Another character at the turn of the twentieth century who tried to earn an honest penny or two was the man who kept a wee coble in the Earl Gray docks. Nicknamed 'Tarry Dan', he got this name because of the liberal amount of tar he would slap on his boat every year. In fact, I wouldn't be surprised if the boat was all tar and no wood.

This redoubtable character would ferry men, women and children around the Earl Gray and King William docks when the dock gates were open at tide times, at the cost of one penny for the round trip of fifteen minutes.

Before the bridges were built at the docks, people had to go round by the Royal Victoria Arch if they wanted to catch one of the many steamers which plied up and down the river. It wouldn't have been a long walk and I can't imagine any long-skirted women climbing into a tiny boat, but that is what they must have done because Dan seemed to make a living out of his mini cruises. However, children on their way to the swimming baths would find this a bit of an adventure.

Of course, the docks and wharves have all gone now to make way for the Tay Road Bridge which was built in 1966. This wouldn't have affected Dan's trade, as he was long gone by this time.

Going to the swimming baths in the 1950s, my

friends and I regularly made our way under the Royal Arch or 'Pigeon's Palace' as it was also known, carrying our 'shivery bite', a wee sandwich or biscuit to eat after coming out of the freezing cold swimming pool.

Oh yes, it was an appropriate name for a snack as I remember being blue with the cold and covered with goose pimples after a session of swimming – or not in my case. I never did get the hang of taking my feet from the bottom of the pool and to this day I still can't swim. That is why, should Tarry Dan still be offering his services, I would have gladly given him a penny just to keep my feet on terra firma.

Thinking about these poor people and hundreds more like them who tried to make a living makes me feel so sad. They must have lived their lives from one financial crisis to another and it was a hard world where no money meant no roof over your head or food to eat. Many of them must have ended up in the poorhouse, which is awful.

My final character, however, was a different person altogether. William Mallachan, who was also known as Tommy Dodds, was a mere four feet in height but what he lacked in inches he more than made up with his intelligence, independence and a quick tongue. Tommy died in 1930 aged seventy-two but he had a fulfilling life. Employed by the boot and shoe emporiums as a messenger he would regularly flog 'the strongest bootlaces ever made.'

He was by all accounts a feisty chappie. A teetotaller, he was often offered drinks by patrons of a local bar, but the barman would put the price of the drink under the counter and Tommy would get it later, in the shape of money. There were no flies on Tommy.

He was also fond of the police force and often, if there was trouble in one of the overcrowded streets, he would give a blast of his police whistle, making sure no one saw who blew the whistle.

The story I love about him was when he met another dwarf in Castle Street. The other wee guy was mesmerised by seeing a double of himself but Tommy took exception to the man's stares and asked him what he was looking at.

I don't know what the man said but there was a boxing bout between the two. A large crowd gathered and it was seemingly so comical to watch. Even the local bobby stood and watched as Tommy emerged the winner although this was because he gave his opponent 'the heid'. Afterwards, no doubt battered and bloody, the man took himself off, back to the Acrobatic Quartette that were performing in the People's Palace.

Tommy, however, was too intelligent to play a comical dwarf for people's entertainment.

On his seventieth birthday, his good friend T. Campbell, who had a hairdresser shop in Gellatly Street, put on a party for him and he received numerous presents.

One of his ploys was to get someone to lay a line of coins on either the floor or the pavement and he would pick them up in his mouth and all done without him bending his legs. I expect he kept these coins as payment for his expertise.

He was a wee man but he never let life make him a

victim. That's what I like about him, he may have been a wee man but he was a wee man with attitude. I just wish I had known him.

And a final word on the swimming baths. One night a friend and I went to visit them, only to be told the last group had gone in for the night and no one else was being admitted. On seeing our faces, the woman on the ticket counter said we still had time to visit the baths.

This must be another swimming pool we thought but we were escorted up the stairs to a row of wooden doors, behind each was a white bathtub. Well we had paid our money so we had to make the best of it.

The laugh was we put on our swimming costumes to get into the bath and although I said nothing at the time, I enjoyed my bath in lovely hot water with a big bar of soap and a lovely towel.

It certainly beat the cold water of the main swimming baths by a million miles, especially when the entire hour had to be spent pretending to swim.

14

The Tay Whale

On one of our many trips to the Albert Institute Museum, my brother and I loved looking at the skeleton of the humpback whale which was caught on the east coast of Scotland in January 1884. Why it travelled into the North Sea is a mystery but it certainly made one big mistake by leaving the deep polar oceans and coming within sight of land at the Tay estuary.

Dundee was the centre of the whaling trade and ships like *The Balena* and *Terra Nova* would sail off to the icy Antarctic in search of whales and seals. At that time, there wasn't the same emphasis on conservation and I'm sure, should a whale appear offshore now, there would be a considerable army of people all trying their best to guide the mammal back out to the deeper waters. But, sadly, not then.

The whale was cruelly harpooned on New Year's Day 1883 and caught in an exhausted condition before finally being landed at Stonehaven on 9 January. I can imagine the excitement of the local population as the huge mammal was finally hauled onto the beach. I don't know if there was considerable interest in buying it but a Dundee man, Mr Johnnie Woods, bought it for £226, a considerable amount of money in those days.

The whale was then transported to the Victoria dock by the tugboat *Excelsior*. It was then put on exhibition behind Johnnie Woods' house in East Dock Street. I think he charged a penny to view the carcass, although I did read somewhere that the admission was sixpence. Whatever, he must have had loads of sightseers because it must have taken a lot of pennies or sixpences to recuperate his initial outlay.

I can imagine the crowds of people who brought their children to see the whale. For people out for a stroll on a Sunday, it must have been the same as going to a local side show and I expect the women would hold handkerchiefs up to their noses, or young courting couples capering near it. The young women maybe protesting, 'Och dinnie push me near it, Bert. Thir's an awfy stink comin aff it.'

By all accounts, thousands of people came to look at the poor dead mammal. Entire families must have had a Sunday outing just to have a look.

Unfortunately, I don't think Mr Woods preserved the carcass because the awful stench soon became unbearable. Not only in Dock Street but also in the surrounding lanes and wynds.

Because of the putrefaction, the whale was then handed over to Professor Struthers of Aberdeen who treated the skeleton.

Afterwards, it was given to the Dundee Museum

where it remains to this day. The sad bones of a magnificent whale that took a wrong turning in the sea have lived on in the memories of the thousands of people who came to view it over many years.

It achieved immortality, which is more than can be said for the thousands of whales and seals that were slaughtered in the cold polar seas by the whaling ships.

15

The All-Singing and Dancing Show

Dancing has always played a big part in the history of Dundee. From the many dance halls like the Palais, Empress, Locarno and Robbie's to the many smaller establishments, patrons have put on their dancing shoes and danced the nights away.

The Palais at 31 South Tay Street opened on 23 July 1938 and was owned by Bertha Wilson and George Dundas. Andy Lothian was a former bandmaster on the Atlantic liner *Athenia*, with his eight-piece band and Harry Rae as a crooner. This liner was torpedoed at the start of the war.

In October 1938, he came to play at the Dundee Palais straight from the Glasgow Empire Exhibition, but with the start of the war he joined the RAF.

Taking his place was bandleader Johnny Lynch who played at Romano's in the Strand but came north because of the blitz.

It must have been wonderful dancing in those days because of all the free gifts given out by various dancehalls. In 1939, if you paid eight visits to the

Palais you got a free wristlet watch. The hall was refurbished in June 1955. I preferred it before refurbishment because of the large squashy settees positioned around the floor. After its makeover, the seating was recessed in the wall and, in my opinion, not so luxurious.

Andy Lothian bought the hall in 1966 and the dancing patrons continued to flock through its doors. How well we all remember dancing to this great band with Jimmy Barton singing 'Davie Crockett' while wearing a racoon hat complete with a tail hanging down. Charlie Coates was the resident crooner while one of the band members with a deep velvet voice sang 'Temptation'. The shivers still run down my back at the memory of it.

The Palais also opened a Sunday night café from 6 p.m. to 9 p.m. Dancing wasn't allowed because it was the Sabbath but how wonderful to have a warm, exciting place to go to on boring, cold winter Sundays. Some patrons who thought they had the talent for singing also got up on the stage, but we mostly preferred the band and sometimes the poor singers were booed off the stage.

The Locarno was the place to be before the war, with Ron Hyatt and his band from the Ritz in Manchester. The band put on a demonstration of the 'Blackpool Walk' and a novice Quick Step competition.

Later, in December 1939, the Locarno was rebuilt and patrons danced to Murray Sheffield and his Dixieland Band. Also on the bill were Monsieur Pierre and Doris Lavelle plus the 'Blackout Stroll'.

Somewhere along the line, the 'Blackpool Walk' seemed to have lost out to the wartime restrictions.

Another dancehall, which opened in December 1938, was the Empress, a detached building which lay in the shadow of the Royal Arch. Owned by Mr and Mrs James Duncan, they also owned the chalet Roadhouse in Broughty Ferry. The bandleader was Carl Volti who was advertised as coming straight from the Ritz in London. Dundee was lucky to get all these wonderful bands from such a prestigious address as the Ritz and no doubt one of the songs played was Fred Astaire's 'Putting on the Ritz'.

What I remember most about the Empress were the big bands who regularly played there during the 1950s and cost a whopping five shillings entrance fee.

At the time I was earning thirty shillings a week so it was a big whack out of my pay packet, but fortunately I had met my future husband by then and he paid for me.

Before going to the dancing it was the custom to go to the Washington Café in the Nethergate and drink a cup of frothy coffee. The café had a great machine that turned the milk into a frothy mass and it was such a novelty for the teenagers of the 1950s. If you shut your eyes you felt you had been transported to downtown America and this bit of frothy coffee pleasure brightened up the years after the war.

Mr Steve Barbieri owned the café the Chrome Rail restaurant as well as the Crystal Bell chip shop in Union Street.

The Chrome Rail had a downstairs restaurant which had a conventional layout but upstairs was totally different. It had a long bar with high stools, lots of black and chrome fittings and a full length mirror along the wall. It was designed to look like an American drugstore.

I worked there for a short time during the summer of 1955. It was a Sunday job and I had been offered it by Mr Alf Wallace who co-owned Wallace's Pie Shop. I believe his daughter was married to Mr Barbieri.

I stuck it out for a few months but I can't say I enjoyed working there. Maybe this was because of the large mirror. It was impossible to turn your back on a customer as they sipped their frothy coffees or milkshakes. If you were cleaning up the worktop, the customers would be staring you in the eyes. But maybe another reason was the fact I was working seven days a week plus two late nights, serving meals at the dinner dances in the Empress ballroom. Perhaps it was all too much.

The only good thing about the job was I could buy a poke of chips from the Crystal Bell chip shop next door on my way home in the evening.

As for the dances, there were other venues like the J. M. Ballroom in Lochee Road, the West End Palais in Well Road, the posh-sounding Continental Ballroom in the Cowgate and the ever-popular Kidd's Rooms in Lindsay Street. I was never a patron of Kidd's Rooms but my husband and his pals were. He has happy memories of spending Saturday nights there.

There was also the Progress Halls on the Hilltown. Nicknamed 'The Progie' it played host to dances every Saturday night and what boisterous affairs they often were.

My pal Annie had a sister who regularly went to these dances. I loved watching her get ready for her evening out. Her dressing table was a wonderful jumble of strange things. To start with she would cleanse her face with Ponds cold cream then slap on the wonderfully titled 'vanishing cream'. I always watched her intently to see if half of her face would disappear but it never did.

Then she would add a thick layer of Max Factor's pancake stick, followed by face powder from a large cardboard box with a huge puff. Finally, putting on deep red lipstick, she would survey herself in the mirror and ask us, 'How dae eh look?' I always thought she looked so glamorous and sophisticated but Annie would reply, 'You look awfy.'

One night, after she had departed for the dance, Annie threw the powder puff in my face and I couldn't see. I gave chase but she darted into the small wardrobe with such force that it toppled over and was only saved from crashing onto the floor by the strong brass bed end.

The door was firmly shut with Annie still inside and I didn't know what to do. Suddenly, deciding to run down to the Progie, I ran out and straight into the burly figure of the downstairs neighbour. 'Whit's that bloody racket you twa are making?' I made some strange strangled noises but he must have understood. He came upstairs with me and managed to get the wardrobe upright but I got such a telling-off by my mum that I was never allowed in the house again when Annie's sister was out.

Another pal had a granny who was always going on

about her expertise on the dance floor. 'Och you should hiv seen me da'en the foxtrot. Abody wanted tae dance wi me.' As I gazed at her, I couldn't visualise this old woman ever being lithe and foxtrotish. To look at her sitting in the sun with her checked slippers and old fringed blanket around her shoulders, it was difficult to imagine, especially as her hobby was now putting her 'horsey' line on. The bookie's runner would appear out of the blue ether and gather these lines. The rule, however, was the punter had to put on a false name on the slip; a nom de plume. 'Eh jist ca' mesel "Ma" but meh lassie up the stairs has delusions o grandeur and signs herself as "Mae West".'

But moving on.

My sister-in-law Ann, although too young to go to the regular dancing, also remembers the times she went to ballet classes. To begin with she went to Miss Watson's classes that were held every Saturday morning in a hall in North Street, but later she joined Jean Pringle's School of Ballet at 9 King Street and was entranced by the dance studio.

Run by Miss Pringle who had been a ballerina, either at Sadler's Wells or Covent Garden, the studio was a delight with its huge windows and a proper barre. Ann recalls loving her class so much that even when confined to bed with 'flu one week, she was so determined to dance at an exhibition, she turned up along with her mother who sat in the front row with a bottle of Lucozade. Ann doesn't recall if she needed it but it was so typical of her mum to be on hand with the first aid.

Dundee has also been a city of song, from the blues

and guitar festivals of today, to the many folk singers and musicians who entertain in the multitude of pubs, not to mention the very talented pop groups.

Playing a large part in this singing tradition are the societies like the Dundee Operatic Society, The Downfield Musical Society, Thomson-Leng Musical Society and Sounds Spectacular.

The Whitehall Theatre plays host to these tuneful groups and their repertoires range from Broadway musicals to show stopping spectaculars. One group of youngsters, judging from their performances in the City Square last year, has such wonderful talent that I wouldn't be surprised if many of them don't end up on the London stage. Calling themselves 'Tread the Boards' their ages range from around five years old up to teenagers. And boy, could they all sing, even the smallest members.

It's great to know that singing and performing is still alive and well in the city that spawned Mary Brookbanks with her famous 'Jute Mill Song', up to the latter day Sheena Wellington.

The Dundee Operatic Society was formed in May or June 1922 and they regularly held their concerts in the King's Theatre in the Cowgate until 1961, when The Whitehall Theatre became the venue for all the concerts and shows. Sadly 1961 was the year when the King's Theatre became a cinema and the stage was removed when the building was refurbished and renamed The Gaumont.

Away back in March 1933, when they were called the Dundee Amateur Operatic Society, they put on the musical *The Desert Song* in the King's Theatre.

On the day of the crucial final rehearsal it was felt that an animal should be in the cast. A camel was out of the question but someone came up with the great idea of having a donkey. A man was found who owned two donkeys so he brought both of them to the theatre. One donkey however was a prima donna, lying down when one of the cast members got on its back. I think the actor tried to approach the animal from every direction but the moment it felt a presence on its back it lay down on the floor, no doubt giving a big hee-haw as an encore.

This donkey was eventually given his marching orders, as the cast didn't want a comical donkey. The requirement was a donkey with acting ability and donkey number two seemed a better possibility. At least he wasn't supine all the time.

The donkey was brought into the wings and gently cantered around with the leading man on his back. So far so good. However, the donkey refused to go on the stage, no matter how much it was coaxed. The star of the show thought a song would help and he sang one of the numbers from the show. No joy.

Appearing onto the scene were some of the cast who were playing French Legionnaires. They decided to manhandle the beast like proper manly legionnaires. With some pulling his head and others shoving his tail, they tried until they were red in the face and the members of the cast had tears in their eyes with laughing. Still no joy.

The stage manager then appeared and he had the great idea to place a carpet between the wings and the stage but this donkey may have been an ass but he wasn't a fool. He remained adamant that the stage wasn't the place to be.

The leading man had another go at cantering around in the wings then made a dash for the stage like some wild-west cowboy, but this ploy was also unsuccessful. Defeat stared them in the face and they gave up. By now everyone who was in the theatre was convulsed with laughter and it must have been a bit of an anti-climax the following night when the show opened. Without the donkey.

The musical societies are still going strong and I wonder if they've had any more animal antics over the years.

It's good to know that the musical and dancing heritage is still going strong. Although the large dance halls of the past are long gone, the Star Ballroom run by Bob and Betty Barty is still surviving.

And there is also disco music to please the young. It may sound loud and discordant to many an older ear but it is still dancing to the sound of music and that can't be a bad thing.

And finally back to *The Desert Song*.

Personally speaking, although it is not recorded which song was sung, I think the star of the show sang the wrong song. Maybe he should have sung 'The Donkey Serenade'. I think the show was a success but it could never have matched the dress rehearsal for drama.

And did the show go on without an animal?

No, they ended up with a pony.

16

The People's Infirmary

Dundee's Royal Infirmary has played a huge part in the lives of the citizens of the city. There can hardly be anyone who hasn't entered its doors since it opened, either as an outpatient, inpatient or a visitor.

The first two-storey infirmary with its two wards was opened in 1798 in King Street where it provided medical accommodation for twenty patients.

The population rose from 30,000 in 1821 to 80,000 in 1851 and because of this expanding growth of people, it soon became clear that the infirmary was too small for all the medical needs of the city.

A new infirmary opened in 1855 in Barrack Road, opposite the Dudhope Park. It had accommodation for 300 patients.

The infirmary depended on charity and donations, and such was the generosity of the jute barons and their families, plus the ordinary man and woman in the street, that a succession of extensions and improvements were added to the original building.

The first ward for children was added in 1883,

Gilroy Home in 1892, Sharp Operating Theatre in 1895, Dalgleish Nurses' Home in 1896, Caird Pavilion in 1907, new Outpatient Department in 1910, a new ENT Department and the Marryat Operating Theatres and X-Ray Department in 1925. The improvements went on for years with the Dudhope House Nurses' home in 1926, the Prain Preliminary Training School for Nurses in 1929, the Sharp Maternity Hospital in 1930, and the Duncan Pathology and Dispensary Building sharing the honours in 1933 with the Eye and Ear Outpatient Department.

The Sidlaw Sanatorium for Children was acquired in 1910 and owing to the terrible scourge of tuberculosis in the city, entire families were afflicted with this disease.

As there was no known cure, patients' beds were put out on open verandas as it was believed that fresh air would cure the disease. Some patients recall wiping snow from the bed covers.

How well I remember the DRI, as my mum was a frequent patient in its wards. I recall reading the plaques above the beds which stated that that particular bed had been donated by some benefactor or other. At the time, I thought the person had donated the actual bed but it wasn't until much later I realised this donation had been a substantial sum of money.

I also recall it was a cavernous place of long corridors, endless staircases and echoing voices. Visiting hours were strict with two visitors per patient and regulated visiting times.

A few years ago, I had the pleasure of meeting

Mrs Alison Kiddie who for many years was a ward sister at the infirmary. This meeting came about through Miss Japp who had been a teacher at Rosebank during my time there and she and Mrs Kiddie were neighbours.

I spent a wonderful afternoon in Mrs Kiddie's flat in Dens Road and she told me all about her time at the DRI. She recalled beginning her training and going to G. L. Wilson's store to buy her pink dress, cuffs, collar and belt, plus a cloak that cost 10/6.

The caps, supplied by the hospital were the Sister Dora type. They also supplied the material for the aprons but the nurses paid for the making up of these garments. The aprons had straps at the back and were about six inches from the floor as it wasn't deemed nice to show a leg.

The nurses were called 'Pinkies' and during a very hot August in 1936, Mrs Kiddie recalls rolling her cashmere stockings down below her knees to keep the air circulating. They also wore sensible, black lacing shoes, which like the rest of the outfit, came from G. L. Wilson's.

When she came to do her second year, she was given her dress but still had to have her aprons made, which had pink stripes. The colours changed with her third year when a navy blue bar was added.

Come the fourth year, and after she passed her SRN, a white band was added and the staff nurses wore grey dresses.

The training took four years in different wards. In the Dudhope House Home, six nurses were admitted every two months and from Monday to Friday there were lectures and tests before spending Saturday and Sunday on the wards. No time off was allowed at this time.

Mrs Kiddie remembers going to the main theatre in 1938 where she remained till the following August. She said it appeared that the hierarchy had forgotten her. She then went on to ward 3 as a staff nurse and later became a sister. She recalled there was a strict rule in the dining room; junior staff couldn't go in front of anyone who was senior and the day started with a call at 6.20 a.m. with breakfast at 7 a.m. and ready for the wards at 7.20 a.m.

The night nurse would have the report ready but there was no sitting down. The report was read and because the night staff didn't go off duty till 8.30 a.m., this nurse and the sister would walk round the ward, noting any admissions during the night.

Time off was erratic, with one morning off once a month or two nights off during night duty. Any nurses who got a Saturday evening off, usually went to church on Sunday morning before reporting for duty at 2 p.m.

Trainee midwives had a harder time of it with few days off in six months. Just one half day off on Sunday once a month.

Mrs Kiddie loved her vocation and one story she told shows her love for the children in her care. One wee lad, who had been seriously ill, stood up in his cot.

'What do you want?' she asked him.

She remembers he squinted at her and said, 'Tea and a take [cake].'

One of her friends was a midwife called Miss Burgess and she recalls her salary when training was £18 a year going up to £36 in year four. She started work at 7.20 a.m. till 9 p.m. with a three-hour break.

She also recalled having to scrape the fluff from the legs of the metal-framed beds. Also, as there was no disposable equipment, everything had to be taken to the sluice room before being sterilised.

After qualifying, she regularly delivered babies in some of the worst slum houses, often ushering out three or four children while their mother gave birth. This led to some hilarious situations.

Some of the children, when being allowed back into the tiny one-roomed flat, would gaze at the new baby, thinking the nurse had delivered it in her black bag. One wee lass met her one day and said, 'Hoo many bairns hiv ye got in yer black bag the day, Missus?'

The infirmary depended on the charity and goodwill of the city and the people didn't let it down, raising money through various means.

Bernard Street, which was a dark narrow street off Hawkhill, regularly put on wonderful displays during royal events. Hundreds of flags and bunting decorated every house and people came from miles around to see it.

On one such occasion, a resident of the street went round with a charity can but he was informed he wasn't allowed to collect money. It must have been against the law or something similar. The disappointed man told the newspaper that the collection was for the Royal Infirmary and he said, 'Nearly abody in the street is grateful for the DRI as maist o the fowk wha live here have been patients there.'

However, the days of charity and donations came to an end with the advent of the National Health Service in 1948 and the scourge of ill health was lifted almost overnight. No longer did anyone have to go without seeing a doctor if they couldn't afford it. Sister Kiddie stayed with her patients during this momentous upheaval and, when she retired, the city honoured her dedication and hard work.

She could recall all the surgeons, doctors and consultants and which branch of medicine they practised, including one that most new mothers of the thirties and forties will recall: Doctor Margaret Fairlie who later became a professor, was Head of Gynaecology and Obstetrics from 1936 onwards.

From the 1920s to the 1940s there were three Matrons: Miss Susan C. McIntosh, 1923–1926, Miss Janet S.H. Nicoll, 1926–1942 and Miss Annie Day, who became the matron in 1943.

Although the infirmary finally closed in the late nineties, the writing was on the wall from 1974 when Ninewells Hospital opened. It was another chapter in the medical scene and just as the King's Road Infirmary closed in the nineteenth century, it was the DRI's turn to shut down in the twentieth century. The building was bought and houses and flats have been built, which means the façade of Dundee's Royal Infirmary hasn't entirely disappeared.

I've never forgotten that afternoon with Miss Japp and Mrs Kiddie. Miss Japp had dedicated her life to teaching her pupils and her pupils loved and respected her, as did the hundreds of patients under Sister Kiddie's care. Now, as they enjoyed their well earned retirement, I saw two ladies with immense strength and both immensely proud of their careers.

Along with Miss Burgess, these three ladies helped babies into the world, taught them at school and cared for them when ill or injured, and this was all done with compassion, humour and hard work.

But to hear them talking about past times that afternoon, it was all remembered with pleasure.

17

Remembering *The Mona*

2009 marks the fiftieth anniversary of the lifeboat, *The Mona*, that foundered with the loss of her eight-man crew. On 8 December 1959 she set off from Broughty Ferry to rescue *The North Carr Lightship*, which was adrift in the North Sea.

It was a wild night with gale force winds as the lifeboat with Ronald Grant, George Smith, James Ferrier, George Watson, Alexander Gall, John Grieve, David Anderson and John T. Grieve answered the call. The Bar which is the dividing line between the river and the North Sea is a dangerous place with treacherous currents and, on this particular night, severe winds.

I remember the following morning vividly. We had not long bought a television set and I was busy doing the ironing when the awful news broke that the crew had all been drowned.

The news stunned the entire city. These men were volunteers, doing a dangerous job over and above their usual jobs and they had been called out on numerous occasions when help at sea was needed, saving hundreds of lives. And now they were all dead. It all seemed so unfair I thought but when was life ever fair?

One of the victims lived in Cotton Road and I regularly walked down this street. I would look at all the windows as I passed, trying to identify the house where I imagined the family would be sitting in their living room, grief-stricken.

The curtained windows gave nothing away and the road looked peaceful and normal. A lot of people volunteered to make up a new team and a replacement lifeboat was launched in 1961 by Princess Marina, the Duchess of Kent. It was called *The Robert*.

The tragedy of *The Mona* brought to attention all the hard, dangerous work carried out by these dedicated volunteers. The people of Dundee and Tayside realised this and they raised a large sum of money for the RNLI. A fund was also set up for the families of the men and, once again, people generously subscribed to it.

Life as they say goes on but fifty years later, there will always be a small corner in the hearts of the Dundee and Tayside people who will never forget *The Mona* lifeboat. Or her crew.

18

A Safe Seat for Life

This was the statement made 100 years ago by Winston Churchill when he was the candidate for Dundee in the 1908 by-election and it was a statement that was to haunt him until his eventual defeat in 1922.

It all started quite well when Churchill was offered the seat after his disastrous defeat in Manchester, owing mainly to the strong Suffragette movement. In fact, it must have been a bitter blow because he had recently been made President of the Board of Trade, which meant he had to seek re-election in order to take up this Cabinet position.

What is inconceivable is the fact he accepted the Dundee seat because if he found the women of Manchester daunting, they had nothing on a city full of working, feisty women. And its Suffragettes were just as militant.

He arrived in Dundee to thousands of people cheering him. He went on to win the election but with such a slender majority that the cheering thousands had obviously not all voted for him.

Elected with him was Sir George Baxter. This was because of the election rules of the day with its double voting system. Also on the candidates list that year was Edwin (Neddy) Scrymgeour, a man who would haunt Churchill all through his Dundee years.

Neddy Scrymgeour was a prohibitionist who stood for the total abstinence of alcohol. It was during this time that Churchill married Clementine Hozier whose mother was Lady Ogilvy, daughter of the Earl of Airlie.

Having a member who was President of the Board of Trade was unpopular in the city. Owing to the high unemployment in the jute and shipbuilding industries, plus the loss of jobs in general, his constituents saw his policies as being detrimental to the main industries in the city.

His popularity was never very high but he managed to hold on to power during the 1910 General Election with the Socialist candidate, Alexander Wilkie coming second.

As the Liberal government at the time had been slashed to a two-seat majority, they decided to hold another election in 1910 and, although Churchill held onto his seat, the country was becoming tired of politics.

Normally, the elections would be held against a barrage of hecklers and people shouting noisily but even they were becoming jaded by the constant campaigning. By now he was Home Secretary but his success in parliament wasn't matched by the grumbles and misgivings of the people of Dundee.

In 1917, Churchill was appointed Minister for

Munitions and as such had to be re-elected. He thought he was the sole candidate but Neddy Scrymgeour stood as a Prohibitionist and Pacifist candidate and it became a contest between the two men.

It was a bitter campaign with both men slagging each other. Neddy accused Churchill of using Dundee to get to better things, while Churchill hit out at Neddy's pacifism. As the country was still at war with Germany and huge losses of life were being reported every day, Neddy's brush with pacifism was to go down like a lead brick.

Neddy was a very sincere man who desperately wanted to close the numerous pubs as drunkenness in the city was rife, and many a household suffered because of it.

However, it was a policy doomed to failure. In spite of his sincerity and popularity as a person, no one wanted the pubs shut and a 'No Change' ballot was recorded twice. Churchill won again in 1918 with Alexander Wilkie coming second with 1,000 fewer votes. But creeping up behind him like some perpetual shadow was Neddy who was increasing his votes with every election.

In 1922, Churchill had an operation to remove his appendix and had to convalesce in London. Clemmie, his wife, did all his campaigning for him. Standing against him were: E. Morel, Socialist; D. Macdonald, National Liberal; R. Pilkington, Liberal; W. Gallacher, Communist, and the ever-present Neddy.

Churchill had been promoted to the War Office; a bad position to be in after the carnage of the First

World War. He had also enforced the Royal Irish Constabulary with men kitted out in khaki uniforms and black belts – the Black and Tans. This group was formed to curtail the violence by the IRA but with Dundee having a massive Irish population, it was a decision that proved very unpopular.

It was also a time of massive unemployment and there had been riots in the city. With hundreds of female jute workers turned away from the Dole Office, the city was in an uproar.

As elections went it was to turn out to be a very bitter one and on the day, the voters turned out in huge numbers.

It must have been like a circus with the Prohibitionists' pipe band marching through the streets as voters hurried to the polling stations.

The result was an outstanding success for Neddy with E. Morel coming second. Churchill lagged in fourth place and never even gave a speech.

It was said at the time that Churchill left the city humiliated and my mother can remember people booing him as he left for the railway station. Churchill was baffled by the apparent hatred of his former constituency and left Dundee for what was to be the very last time. At the time he said that he 'would live to see the grass grow over the city's jute mills.'

This statement was probably treated with disdain. After all, Britain had an empire on which the sun never set and Dundee had its jute mills on which the doors would never close. Although it was a prophecy that didn't come true for many many years, it did indeed come to pass.

Yet it had all started so well back in 1908 but Churchill's finest hours were still to come and the country would have a lot to be grateful for when he became the war leader and stood up to Hitler and the Nazis. One of his quotes at the time of the Munich Crisis, when he defended his policy not to negotiate with Hitler, was, 'You can't appease a crocodile with words.'

What is strange is why he didn't seek a better seat nearer London, one with people like his 'ain kind'; people who moved in political circles and lived like the Churchills in their big houses. The city of Dundee had a population blighted by unemployment, social deprivation, poor overcrowded housing and voters who weren't afraid to speak their minds. Not to mention feisty women.

Back in London he must have ruminated on his statement of 'an easy seat' because it turned out to be a pill too bitter to swallow. Neddy went on in politics but never managed to get his prohibitionist law through Parliament and he stayed as candidate for Dundee until 1931.

Dingle Foot, who was a Liberal, and Florence Horsburgh, a Unionist, beat him. Miss Horsburgh was the first ever female Member of Parliament for Dundee and she was able to deal with rowdy hecklers and people out to cause mayhem.

It was still a time of very high unemployment for the country and Dundee, in particular, with over 26,000 people on the dole. It was a tough life for voters and parliamentary members alike, but they were both re-elected in 1935. Both of them served in

Winston Churchill's coalition government during the war but 1945 was to see the biggest turnaround in the government.

The Labour party had two contestants in this election, T. Cook and John Strachey. Also standing for the very first time was an SNP candidate, Arthur Donaldson.

The results were to be catastrophic for Churchill's government with Clement Attlee's party with its Welfare State manifesto proving to be what the people wanted. The country was tired of wars and shortages, rationing and unemployment, ill health and bad housing.

Dingle Foot and Florence Horsburgh lost their seats to the two Labour men. How well I remember this election in Dundee. As children we would run around the streets chanting: 'Vote, vote, vote for Mr Strachey. He's the man wha'll gie ye ham and eggs. If ye dinnie vote for him then he'll brak yer windies in and ye'll nivver see yer windies oany mair.' What windows had to do with ham and eggs was a mystery but we all enjoyed going around shouting it out.

As it turned out, Mr Strachey never managed to give us ham and eggs and he even rationed bread for the very first time, but times were difficult and the government weren't miracle workers. One good thing to come out of this 1945 government was the National Health Service that still looks after our health sixty years on.

Elections don't seem to have the same fire in them now. Not like the days when Dundee must have seemed like a frontier town to Churchill. It was probably because so many people ventured out on the streets and it would seem like a good idea to pack into halls and give the candidates holy hell. No doubt they left the halls buzzing with excitement and having a jolly good entertaining night out. How the poor candidates felt like is another story.

19

The Octocentenary Jamboree

1991 saw the 800th birthday of Dundee and the city was determined to celebrate this milestone.

Henny King, a Canadian from Montreal, was made the director of this momentous occasion and although there was some criticism of her post, she was more than able fore the job, organising events that culminated in the giant street party on Saturday 1 June 1991. Thousands of people turned out on that sunny June day to take part or just to be spectators. It was a spectacular day of brilliant sunshine that started off with Lord Provost Tom Mitchell, with Ron Coburn acting as Dundee's Bellman, leading the crowd in a rousing 'H .ppy Birthday'.

Then on with the show. Entertainment was on a large scale: artistes who showed the extent of different cultures in the city from a Chinese dragon; Wurzburg's Rhonrad Wheels with their giant steel hoops; fly-past of jet planes from RAF Leuchars, and the Black Watch Pipe Band, who were Freemen of the City.

Also taking part along with groups from the city's churches, the fire-juggling unicyclists and all the various bands who played music almost non-stop, were Ye Amphibious Ancients, wonderful, hardy people who swim in the icy River Tay and who make the regular special dip on New Year's Day.

The street party continued into the evening with torch-bearers wearing masks depicting mythical animals that were supposed to represent the city. All I can say is I'm glad these animals weren't roaming the streets of my childhood, but it was all good fun.

The torch-bearers were part of the Elephant and Whale *son et lumière* show and there was a wonderful firework display to round off the day. What saddened me on the day was the fact that most of the old city had been razed to the ground and concrete and glass boxes were standing proudly in their place.

Dundee, like many other cities has a history of bloodshed and tragedy as a result of the many times it has been conquered by, mostly English, forces. The city was sacked and burned to the ground by various armies in 1303 and 1548.

The last battle was when Oliver Cromwell's Roundhead army, led by General Monck, laid siege to the city for eight days before finally capturing it on 1 September 1651. It was estimated that a fifth of the population including women and children were slaughtered and were all buried in a mass grave. The city was left in ruins that lasted for many years.

This all came about because of the coronation of Charles II, which took place at Scone on New Year's Day 1651. He led a Scottish army to a disastrous defeat at Worcester and because of Dundee's support for the king, this slaughter was Cromwell's retaliation.

General Monck's headquarters at this dreadful time was a house at the foot of the Overgate. Centuries later and for reasons unknown, the city's councillors of the day seemed determined to erase the old city and replace everything with modern buildings. Now I'm not denying some of the old houses needed to be demolished but entire swathes of medieval streets were bulldozed; streets like the Wellgate and Overgate. The Overgate in particular was turned into a grey, bleak, windswept shopping mall with as much personality as a lump of concrete.

On the day of the party, all signs of General Monck's house with its distinctive tower and staircase, had been replaced by the frontage of Littlewoods department store. Not that there was anything wrong with the shop, but it could have been built anywhere.

Also gone was the Sixty-Minute Cleaners; a business that was situated under General Monck's house. I often wondered if they ever cleaned any garment in an hour because I recall having to wait a few days for a dress. But maybe I was unlucky.

One part of medieval Dundee has fortunately survived. In 1564, land was gifted to the city by Mary Queen of Scots and this later became the Howff Graveyard, which for years was the meeting place of the Nine Incorporated Trades of Dundee.

Several years on from the birthday bash, Dundee has regained some pride in her heritage and the people in power are finally waking up to conservation instead of demolition.

The Wellgate and Overgate although sadly missed now have well-designed shopping malls. The Overgate is especially pleasing with its huge windows overlooking the most ancient building of the city, the Auld Steeple.

Soaring into the sky, the steeple is the remaining part of the old St Mary's Church which was founded in the twelfth century, but was a casualty of all the carnage left by the various armies until Monck's army finally left it in ruins. However, St Mary's Church, now known as the City Churches, was restored in the nineteenth century.

The homecoming of *Discovery*, the ship which took Captain Scott and his crew to the South Pole, has also contributed to the regeneration of Dundee.

Dundee, now into the second decade of its ninth century, has seen many changes. The old industries of whaling, jute and shipbuilding have vanished. New ones which replaced them, factories like Timex, NCR, Valentines, Astral, Vidor Batteries and the other factories of the Industrial Estate of the 1940s are also long gone. But, as away back in 1191, the people of Dundee remain the city's best asset and that's the way it should be.

Buildings and armies fade away but people stay the same. That is why an estimated 50,000 people were out in the streets to celebrate Dundee's historic milestone on that wonderful hot and sunny day in June 1991.

20

Market Days

Dundee is a city of markets, going back to Lady Mary's Fair and the Greenmarket which were held in the shadow of the Vault, a medieval collection of houses and shops that the building of the Caird Hall has long since erased.

In its heyday the Greenmarket was a mecca for the shopper looking for household goods or any other item of bric-a-brac, from chipped ornaments to items of furniture. My grandad sometimes had a site here but what he sold was never recorded. What was recorded was my mother's annoyance at having to look after the collection of items on sale. I recall her telling me that she hated having to haggle with any potential customers and keep an eye on any would-be pilferer, not to mention having to sit out in all weathers, as this market wasn't undercover. Goods for sale were laid out on the ground and customers could take in at a glance what was on offer and a lot of it was either tatty or well-worn. I don't recall if she ever mentioned her brother, my Uncle Charlie, taking a turn. But knowing grandad, he more than likely did.

The Greenmarket finally stopped trading in 1934 but as one site closed down, another popped up somewhere else.

A great trip on a Saturday was to the stalls at Mid Kirk Style, a narrow lane that ran between South Lindsay Street and Tally Street, and was bordered on one side by the wall of the Old Steeple. This was a popular place to be because this market was home to the famous Buster Stall, that ambrosial dish of chips, peas and vinegar.

Like the Greenmarket, vendors just placed their wares either on old wooden barrows or on the street. Some enterprising sellers had the foresight to have a piece of tarpaulin over their goods but more often than not, they were left out in all kinds of weather, rain, snow or wind.

This market closed down in 1957 when the Overgate was demolished, but before this happened, another small market was held on spare ground beside Long Wynd. I loved this market because it sold a mixture of really old things and brand new items.

I read somewhere that one vendor regularly sold old spectacles from a large suitcase. Customers tried them out by looking at a newspaper and if the print was readable then a purchase was made. Where was the sense in paying for an eye test when there were so many spectacles to choose from the suitcase?

Nylon stockings were very difficult to get after the war but by the early 1950s they began to appear for sale. On one occasion I was at a stall with scores of packets of nylons on sale. There was a huge crowd of women all clamouring to buy these wonderful sheer stockings and I was one of them.

I was sixteen with very little money but the salesman, a man with a glib patter and his eye on making a quick half crown, persuaded me to part with my hard-earned cash. I should have been a bit more on the ball when he kept asking everyone who made a purchase if they were happy with it. There were to be no returns he said, or any cash given back.

Feeling a bit alarmed by this insistence, I turned the cellophane packet over in my hands and everything appeared to be just hunky-dory, until, when trying them on at home, I found that although the stockings were fine, the seam and the heel were only finished on one side. In those days, stockings had a seam and a shaped brown heel at the ankle, but one side was brown and the other unfinished.

Viewing the stockings from the left they looked perfect but from the right they looked odd and it was worse from the rear as it made your legs look misshapen. My mother roared with laughter when she saw them and said, 'Aye thir's aye some spiv ready to sell duds.' Or words to that effect.

Like Queen Victoria, neither the spiv nor my mother's derision amused me. I tried to make the best of a bad bargain. 'Och eh dinnie think fowk will notice,' I said hopefully. This brought another burst of mirth. 'Naebody will notice. Hivvens they mak yer legs look squint.'

Well, that was it. I wasn't going around with squint legs, nylons or no nylons, so they went in the bin. I kept going back to that market but the stocking man was never seen again.

After the demise of Mid Kirk Style, another market opened in Dens Road. This one was situated in a building and the days of tea sets and clothes lying out in the elements were long gone as there were proper stalls that enabled the vendor to artistically exhibit their goods.

And there was a Buster Stall.

One market I was only ever in once was Craig Street, also known as 'Paddy's Market'. Perhaps I picked the wrong day but it was full of foreign sailors from boats in the docks and I thought everything had a mouldy smell. I was with a friend and we both made a quick exit.

Dundee was also full of second-hand shops that stocked piles of clothes and old shoes but these shops are no longer with us. They've metamorphosed into upmarket charity shops with loads of great bargains.

I've often wondered who puts out such good clothes, shoes, handbags and household goods. I know it isn't me because I'm like a squirrel and have things dating back years when I was a size 12. And that wasn't yesterday.

As a child, I remember the travelling 'cutler'. He had a little wagon and people brought their knives and axes to be sharpened. I would stand watching him and the sparks would fly into the air and there was the sharp rasping noise as metal met stone. We never used his services but he must have had a clientele because he appeared regularly, parking his wagon outside the Plaza Picture House.

Although not in Dundee, one market I remember very well is the Barras in Glasgow. Like Craig Street, I've only visited it once but on that occasion I got such a laugh that I've never forgotten it.

On that Saturday morning, there had been torrential rain and we quickly skirted around the open air stalls. On one stall was a clothes rack filled with fur coats and they were soaking wet. Suddenly the sun came out in the afternoon and I couldn't believe my eyes as the fur began to dry out, sending huge steams of moisture and the smell of moth balls into the air.

I had just made the remark about what idiot would ever consider buying a sodden wet fur coat when this wee woman started trying them on. It was so funny when she began to pick her way through the selection in order to find her size. 'Eh cannie see meh size here, son. Dae ye hiv oanything thit will fit me?'

The stallholder began to rummage along the row and finally produced this apparition that resembled a shaggy brown bear. The woman loved it and then tried to haggle a price with the man. Not once was the wet fur or the mouldy smell mentioned and she went away quite happy with her purchase.

Now, when I view the hygienic and squeaky-clean farmer's market stalls or the exotic smells from the continental markets, I recall the steaming wet fur coat.

Nothing, but nothing could ever top that.

21

Crossing the River

The River Tay's origins are in the hills beyond Loch Tay and it sweeps down through small towns and rural meadows until it reaches Perth, and then beyond to Dundee and the North Sea.

On 18 August 1966, after years of deliberations and setbacks, a road bridge was built over the river from Dundee to Fife. W. A. Fairhurst designed the bridge and the original plans for the bridge are still kept with the firm. The main contractor was Duncan Logan Ltd and Willie Logan was the man on the spot, overseeing the subcontractors and the general daily construction of the bridge.

It brought many jobs to Dundee and on the opening day when the late Queen Mother cut the ribbon and was then driven over in style, the route was lined with hundreds of spectators, workers with their families and friends plus many people from the city who wanted to see a milestone in history.

But like all dangerous work, the bridge wasn't built without tragedy and three men were drowned when a temporary section fell into the river. Then there was the sad, untimely death of Willie Logan. All the celebrations on the day, when the late Queen Mother officially declared the bridge open, must have been heartbreaking for the families of these men. Just looking at all the flags and colourful displays must have brought back all their unhappy memories.

The new road bridge also heralded the demise of the beloved Fifies; those flat-bottomed boats that regularly ferried people and vehicles over the water. For many years these ferries were used for pleasure trips over to Newport and they played a huge part in my young life. George and I were devotees of this form of transport and many happy days were spent on the water. Mum however was a bit lukewarm about crossing the river. She never like being near water.

On that last day, *The Scotscraig* was bedecked with flags and many passengers crossed over to Fife to be met by hundreds of people who had all come to the pier at Newport to say farewell to an old friend. They all joined in singing 'Auld Lang Syne' and the return journey saw passengers dancing.

The bridge has gone from strength to strength as the car-owning population has grown year by year since 1966 and thousands now cross every day. The poor Fifies would have sunk under this onslaught and it's true that the old must give way to the new. Just as the old fateful railway bridge with its tragic history gave way to a better designed and safer bridge.

Dundee is blessed with a beautiful waterfront with the long walk of the Esplanade leading up to the magnificent structure of the Tay Railway Bridge, sweeping in a gentle curve to the shores of Fife on the opposite side

Up until 1870, crossing the river was done by steamers that regularly sailed between Dundee and Sea Myles, latterly known as Newport. 1870 was the year Parliament agreed on the building of a railway bridge and, at over two miles long, was at the time the longest bridge in the world.

Engineer Thomas Bouch designed the bridge and work began in 1871. The first problem that Bouch encountered was his mistake in thinking there was a foundation of solid rock when, instead, there was only sand. This meant that the bridge had to be redesigned.

The building of the bridge was fraught with danger and many men lost their lives. One terrible accident stands out. On 27 August 1873, a quarter mile from shore, six men were working on pier 54 when they were trapped in a shaft and drowned. James Gellately, Charles Thomson, Alexander Clelland, James Herd, W. Stewart, and John Denholm all lost their lives that day and ten children were made fatherless.

Another incident, which fortunately didn't result in deaths, was in February 1877 when, during a fierce storm, fifty-four workmen were marooned overnight. The storm caused a lot of damage and with hindsight, it was a taste of what was to come.

The bridge however opened on May 1878 with the designer, now Sir Thomas Bouch, crossing in triumph. A triumph that didn't last long.

On the night of 28 December 1879, there was a gale blowing which reached force eight or nine as the northbound train from Edinburgh reached St Fort Station. The tickets were collected here but there were at least five children on board who didn't need a ticket. There were also two young adults, Margaret Kinnear aged seventeen and James Peebles aged fifteen.

The train set off across the bridge and while it was within the high girders, this section broke off and took the girders, train and passengers into the dark, cold waters of the Tay.

It's not hard to imagine the panic-stricken thoughts of those poor people. Passengers like Robert Watson and his two small sons, David and Robert aged six and nine, Mr Neish from Lochee and his five-year-old daughter Bella, and Elizabeth Brown aged fourteen who was travelling with her grandmother Elizabeth Mann. Then there were brothers Alex and William Robertson, who had visited their parents at Abernethy, Mrs Meldrum who left a family of six, Councillor Jobson, and brother and sister, Archibald and Jessie Bain.

The saddest ones were the passengers who got on the train so close to the bridge, at St Fort; James Peebles; George Johnstone and his fiancée Eliza Smart, who was a niece to Annie Cruickshanks, another passenger on the train. Then there was Mrs Cheap who left a grown-up family, Alice Upton aged sixteen and William Macdonald along with his eleven-year-old son David.

Another sad tale which makes one wonder if there is such a thing as destiny was the journey of two ladies, Mrs Easton and Annie Cruickshanks. Mrs

Easton was the niece of Lady Baxter of Edinburgh and Annie was a housemaid at the house. The tragedy was that both ladies should have travelled on an earlier train but the cabbie that had been hired to take the fare to the station slept in which meant they took the later train.

The first items to be washed ashore were mailbags on Broughty Ferry beach and out of a total of forty-six bags, thirty-seven were recovered and the mail delivered, which sounds a bit gruesome but these were different times. Debris from the carriages was also soon washed up on Broughty Ferry beach.

The first passenger to be found at Tay Grove, East Newport was unknown until Elizabeth Cruickshanks identified her sister Annie Cruickshanks, the housemaid from Edinburgh.

More debris was washed ashore, drivers' caps and flags, a muff, a black lace shawl, and a travelling bag, which was later identified as belonging to Mr Robert Sime, who was a clerk at the Royal Hotel. Also found was a box containing fruit knives and forks; no doubt a gift from one of the passengers to someone special.

The inquiry, which was held a few days later didn't hear all the facts and as a result the hurricane was blamed, and because Thomas Bouch admitted he hadn't allowed for this, the wind factor was considered the main reason for the disaster.

What didn't come out at the time was the fact that two of the girders had fallen into the river during the bridge's construction. One was damaged beyond repair but the second one was lifted and straightened and deemed suitable for use. Unlike today, engineering experts in Victorian times didn't understand the theory of straightening metal and the damage it could cause. At the time of this fateful decision, it was touch and go if the girder was to be used or scrapped. What a great pity the argument for saving it won. There was also evidence that the iron used for the girders was flawed with holes being filled up and painted over.

Also known at the time but never mentioned at the inquiry was a kink in the rail. This kink in the rail was in the girder which had been damaged and reports that the 5.50 p.m. train from Tayport, the train before the ill-fated one, had seemingly had a rough journey shows that damage to the bridge was evident. Nothing however was noticed.

Another fault was that the bridge was liable to suffer from vibrations and the tie bars were seemingly snapping before that final and fateful journey.

One of the theories put forward, when the reports from the disaster were opened to the public, was that the second-last carriage became derailed by the kink in the line and by the time the train reached the fifth girder, a disaster was inevitable.

One of the divers found debris from the train near Wormit and much further away from where the train was eventually located, which looked as if this carriage had suffered from derailment and was running along the wooden floor instead of on the line.

What must the thoughts of these passengers have been like as they realised they were in trouble? It must have been pure panic. At the time they wouldn't have realised they were trapped in a cage as both the train and girders fell into the river. This was proved right when the girders were raised and the engine was still trapped inside.

Then there was the rumour that there was a terrible injury to the stoker who suffered a badly-burned face where he had hit the hot boiler and this gave credence to the theory of a derailed train.

As the derailed carriage slammed into the rest of the train, the engine must have come to a halt with a severe jolt. What came out at the inquest was that the train hadn't put on its brakes or that the steam hadn't been shut off which led to the conclusion of the train coming to grief before the driver could do anything.

Looking back, it's all 'perhaps' or 'if'. Perhaps if the broken tie bars had been noticed in time, and if the terrible storm had been taken into consideration, then maybe the train would not have entered the bridge. But it was dark outside and the damage went unnoticed, with the passengers riding on to their fateful ends.

There were sixty passengers on board including seven children. Only forty-seven bodies were ever recovered. Thirteen were never found.

The next day the full damage was seen. Thirteen girders were no more. They were lying on the bottom of the river and a huge gaping hole in the middle of the bridge was viewed with sorrow and consternation by crowds of people who thronged the Esplanade to see the carnage.

Like every disaster there were stories of fortunate escapes; about people who should have been on the train but for some reason or another were not. A married couple who were on their honeymoon in Edinburgh were at a party on the Sunday afternoon but were persuaded to stay over because of the storm. Then there was Mr J. T. Chatterton Baxter and two friends who got off the train at St Fort. Because of the storm, the three men didn't want to travel over the bridge and they stayed the night at Newport when they found out that no steamers were running.

Another lucky escape was a soon-to-be bridegroom who was a carpenter in the Merchant Service, who had travelled over to Newport for a few drinks. This chap was very superstitious and always carried a baby's caul or birth cap for good luck and protection.

When he found out there were no steamers running because of the weather, he made his way to the St Fort station. He was almost on the train when the stationmaster stopped him going aboard because of his inebriation. He was carrying his caul as usual and it certainly looks as if it saved his life.

As the days went on and the hardship of the families began to bite, a concert was organised for the Tay Bridge Disaster Fund. This was held in the Kinnaird Hall in Bank Street on Friday, 6 February 1880. It was an evening of Scotch music and Burns songs with sopranos, Mrs Hamilton Nimmo and Miss Nellie Wallace, contraltos, Miss Maggie Wallace and Mrs H. Crooks, tenors, Mr J. B. Macdonald and Mrs A. Swirles, baritones, Mr J. Addison Kidd and Mr A. E. Adams. Bass was Mr Robert Ferguson.

Admission to the front seats and the gallery was four shillings, second seats two and sixpence, and the area one shilling. The concert began at 7.45 p.m. and as a measure of the well-to-do audience, carriages were to be at the door at 10 p.m. to take people home. I hope they raised lots of money for all the poor families left without a breadwinner. The grief must have been unbearable but to be also destitute would have been terrible.

What made it even more poignant was the fact that it was almost the New Year holiday, a time when people were travelling to see friends and family and that was what the majority of the passengers were doing. Little did they know they were saying their last goodbyes.

Of course, it's all past history now, nearly 130 years ago and there have been numerous other disasters with bigger losses of life but this was Dundee's disaster and as such it has seeped into the psyche of the Dundee people. They may not think about it very often but it lies in the background, a terribly sad catastrophe for the doomed souls on the train and the many deaths that resulted from building the rail and road bridges over the dangerous waters of the River Tay.

22

Happy Birthday *Beano*

I was in a newsagent's the other day and saw an advert for a paperboy or girl, morning only deliveries with the grand wage of twenty-seven pounds a week with a bonus. I mentioned to the owner that, should I have lived nearer the shop, I would have applied for the job. 'If you did apply for the job I would employ you right away. I can't get anyone to do the job and the vacancy has been in the window for weeks,' she said.

I forgot to ask about the bonus but it brought back to mind my paper round about fifty-eight years ago. At the time I felt so fortunate to get this job as there was a great deal of competition around as youngsters scrambled to make some money.

I worked for Mr Hynd who owned the shop on Strathmartine Road and dead on six-thirty every morning I was at the shop collecting my huge bag of papers. My round took me to the top of the Hilltown, up Hill Street and in a giant sweep around Byron Street, plus all the interconnecting streets in between. And it wasn't the case of throwing the paper at the front door. I had to trudge up and down flights of stairs, often in the dark. Then I headed back homewards towards Moncur Crescent, pushing the last *Courier* through the letter box of the top floor flat in the close next to the Plough Bar.

This routine went on for about a week or so until my final customer complained to the shop owner:

> Eh dinnie get meh paper until half past seven and eh'm on meh way tae work. Eh like tae read meh paper wi meh porridge and eh'm running doon the stairs when eh see the paper lassie swanning up the stairs as if she's got the hale morning tae deliver it.

Mr Hynd duly noted the complaint and told me not to 'swan aroond' and to make sure I started my round with the complainer. Now I don't know what job this guy did but if he thought delivering a huge bag of newspapers was swanning around then he should have exchanged jobs with me. But I did as I was told and the customer who used to be first on the round was now the last. Thankfully he or she didn't complain and I was extremely grateful to them, but maybe they didn't like getting porridge on their paper.

After school, it was the same laborious round with the *Evening Telegraph*, always making sure the grumpy guy got his 'Tele' with his tea.

The weekends were really hard as there was another delivery on Saturday evening with the *Sporting Post*. This was usually a small bundle but the customers were as far flung which meant it still took as long to get around.

Then there was Sunday morning. The bag was so

heavy that I had to make three trips to the shop in order to deliver to all the extra customers I had. My round was further afield on a Sunday and I couldn't understand it. Thankfully, in the 1950s the Sunday papers weren't so thick as they are now, but the customer list seemed huge.

The answer was soon solved when I overheard one of the other paper girls telling her friend that her mother wouldn't let her work on a Sunday, but she still got the same money as before. I was so aggrieved at this unfairness because I was also still getting the same money as before, but was now doing a lot more for it. But my mother needed the money and there was nothing I could do about it except simmer with annoyance.

I was good at simmering as I trudged through rain and snow that winter, my hands feeling numb from the cold or else getting soaked, my feet squelching in my waterlogged shoes as I climbed umpteen stairs and almost lost fingers with some of the snappy letter boxes.

I often wondered if the letter boxes matched the owners, some being so large and generous that a bus could have slipped through, while others were so thin and mean-looking that it took all my expertise to push the paper through. If there was more than one paper going through, I had to feed them in one by one where they landed behind the door with a satisfying plop and hopefully not spreadeagled all over the lobby lino.

Still there was one perk. I got to look at the comics before putting them through the door. Just a quick look as I hurried along the streets but how I enjoyed reading in the *School Friend* comic about the Four Marys who were in a boarding school and, dressed in hooded robes, had wonderful experiences with mysteries. It all seemed so marvellous and a thousand light years away from Rockwell Secondary where I was a pupil.

Then there were *The Beano*, *The Dandy*, *The Hotspur* and *Adventure* and I would lap up Lord Snooty and Desperate Dan but my all time favourite was Keyhole Kate. I loved her sharp nose which I imagined would always be twitching.

Some customers also bought the *Red Letter*, *True Romances* and *Secrets* magazines and, if it was a sunny day and if I had time, I would read the first story in these romantic, forbidden papers. They were actually quite tame but I didn't realise that at the time.

Then there was Dixon Hawke in the *Sporting Post*, a detective in the police force who managed to solve a crime every week with no bother.

I was always careful to make sure I didn't damage or crease my reading matter because I couldn't afford to have another grumpy customer running off to the shop to complain.

With hindsight, I realise now that I was the willing horse who was always being asked by the owner of the shop to do the extra runs and maybe in some eyes that smacked of exploitation, but quite honestly I didn't know the meaning of the word away back then, so ignorance was bliss. And at the end of the week I had my few shillings. I can't remember the exact amount, I think it was three and sixpence or it may have been just under five shillings. Now this may sound a lot but not when all the miles I walked was taken into account plus the heavy bags to carry.

One Christmas I remember vividly was when our Uncle Charlie arrived with a present for my brother and me. He also had a big pile of *Film Fun* and *Girl's Crystal* comics. To this day I can't recall what the gift was but I've never forgotten the comics. We pounced on them with such glee that it could have been treasure from some secret locked room investigated by the Four Marys.

Such was the power of comics and although some are no longer in existence, *The Dandy* and *The Beano* are still going strong. *The Dandy* was seventy years old in 2007 while *The Beano* celebrated its seventieth birthday on 30 July 2008. Although I never knew it away back in 1938, I almost have the same birthday. Just one day out.

During all these years, both comics have given children so much pleasure. From Big Eggo to Biffo the Bear. Korky the Cat to Desperate Dan with his gigantic cow pie complete with a pair of horns, and Lord Snooty and his pals.

So Happy Birthday *Beano*.

I wish I had aged as well as you have.

23

The Tattie Gatherers

After the war, getting the potato harvests gathered in was a priority and schoolchildren were drafted in every autumn to do the picking. Aged thirteen and in my second year at Rockwell, the entire class was asked to put their names down for this three-week harvest. We got the impression the teachers weren't happy with this arrangement but it was a case of 'Your Country Needs You'.

I don't think it was compulsory but the majority of us were eager to be out of the classroom and I think there were only one or two pupils who didn't go.

The ones who did go from all the classes would gather in the assembly hall of the school and be allocated a place on a bus before being whisked away to *the country*; that unknown place, at least as far as I was concerned.

I always thought we were going to the middle of nowhere as the bus drove along miles of rural roads with hardly any houses to be seen and, more importantly, no shops, but after what seemed hours on the bus we would pull in at a secluded field and we would all troop off.

My first year at the tatties coincided with sharp frosts and lovely sunny days but the sight of rows of tattie shaws stretching for miles certainly lowered our high spirits. All the way there, we would all chat about the remote possibility of finding a dwarfish grieve with tiny legs but when the said grieve appeared, he was always over six feet in height with huge long legs encased with twine bindings around his trousers.

We stood in a huddle as he strode over the frost-encrusted field, marking out our 'bit', either placing a twig or marking the ground with his huge heel, his feet gouging the earth. He said, 'Noo that's yer bittie and mind and pick aw the tatties an no leave ony.'

Sheila, my schoolfriend and I would look in dismay, as the 'bittie' seemed to stretch to eternity, but we waited dutifully with our wire baskets for the tractor to appear. A murmur would go round. 'Eh hope it's a digger wiv got and no a scatterer,' but it was always a scatterer attached to the tractor and a groan would be heard.

The scatterer was self-explanatory; it scattered the tatties over a wide area while the digger left them in a neat row. It was a case of zigzagging from side to side as well as picking the tatties in front of you, and there were always some that were shy, hiding in mounds of cold frosty earth with just the tips showing.

Running back and forth gathering these hidden tatties took time and there was hardly any time to

109

straighten up before the tractor was chugging up behind us with the bogie ready to hold the gathered tatties.

Sometimes some of the boys were wicked and pushed these half hidden tatties back into the earth with their feet but comeuppance time would surely come around at harrowing time, when we would walk behind the harrower like animals in Noah's Ark.

We trailed around the field two by two, carrying a wire basket between us, this machine uncovering all the tatties left behind by the pickers.

There was a small break in the middle of the morning and we all flopped down between the dreels and had our snack. Mine was always a roll in jam and some lemonade which tasted ambrosial. It was also the time to try and get some feeling back in your hands as howking the tatties out of the cold earth always left your fingers numb with cold. I don't know if many of the pickers wore gloves. I know I didn't.

At dinner time we were bussed to a local school or hall to have our hot dinner and all I can recall of these meals was that it always seemed to be mince and tatties, but no one was complaining as we were all starving.

At one hall there was an outside tap to wash your hands and the water was freezing. Trying to get your hands clean was a job and a half, but no one was particularly worried about a few dirty fingernails.

Except Dora. Her meal must have always been cold by the time she sat down because she would scrub her nails with a tiny brush and then take out a small manicure set and proceed to file them. She then continued with a vigorous brushing of her hair before tying a scarf around her head, gypsy fashion.

Some of the girls wore woollen scarves under their jackets but I think she was the only one who wore a scarf over her hair. The rest of us were quite happy to shake the earth out of our tresses, and the little stones that had been thrown up by the scatterer. To say I was impressed by this beauty routine was an under-statement and I made up my mind to save up for a manicure set.

Later, as the sun began to go down, the grieve would walk up the length of the field and shout, 'It's lousing time.' Not being acquainted with rural speak, I hadn't a clue what he was saying but thank the Lord he was saying it was time to finish.

Then we would all pile onto the bus for the home-ward journey with some of the boys singing popular tunes with smutty lyrics. Without thinking one day, I was singing one of these songs and my mother almost choked on her biscuit that she was eating at the time.

The lyrics were quite harmless really, especially when viewed in this more liberal time, but back in the 1950s, my mum thought it was terrible. I had to promise not to listen to the songs, but that would have been a hard task as the boys, being macho, always belted them out.

The routine then began again the next morning and lasted for three weeks. If I loved the tattie picking then Mum was ecstatic with the wages of eleven and thruppence a day. It was almost a fortune in our house.

Our class went back the following year and the same routine was carried out, travelling all over Angus and Perthshire to do our bit for the essential tattie gathering.

I expect it was the same in the autumn of 1953 but I had departed the school by then to go on to pastures new. And I never did save up for a manicure set.

24

It Begins with a 'B' but it's Not Butlins

Mention the word holiday camp and people immediately think of Butlins famous camps after the war. Billy Butlin catered for the growing army of people who longed for a bit of glamour after the war years and, from the late 1940s onwards, going to Butlins was the epitome of many holidaymakers' dreams.

Crammed with entertainment on a grand scale and scores of fun-packed days filled with knobbly knees and glamorous granny competitions, a fun time was promised to all. The happy campers had wonderful shows to see, posh dance halls and theme bars to drink and dance in, and the ever-present 'Redcoats' to oversee their every whim.

I never went to Butlins but, in 1950, I did go to Belmont Camp at Meigle with the primary seven class of Rosebank School.

We were taken by bus to this holiday camp and it was situated in the middle of a forest. At least that was where I think it was because as far as I was concerned it seemed to be in a clearing with a forest all around it.

There were wooden type buildings with dormitories for the boys and girls, a dining hall and schoolrooms. We did our lessons in the morning and nature study and country pursuits in the afternoon. We were taken around the woods, identifying different trees and flowers, squirrels and beetles and general wildlife. Then there were the country walks. One teacher I recall was an ex-military man and he would take us on three-mile walks that took us up to the hotel by the railway bridge and back again.

He didn't allow any dawdling either. It was strict march-time the entire way and we were all tired by the time we got back to base. Well maybe not everyone but I know I was.

Like in Butlins camp, we all ate in a large communal dining room and for some reason the meal I recall best was supper, when we all drank a big cup of cocoa and ate thick slices of buttered bread.

On Sunday we were marched again to the church but I don't recall visiting any shops in the village, which was just as well as I don't think anyone had much money. There was a tuck shop on site. It was quite well stocked because sweet rationing had ended the previous year in April 1949.

The postman delivered letters to the camp and one morning as I was sitting in the classroom, I almost fell off my chair when I was handed two letters. One was from my father, who must have been in one of his erratic contacts with my Mum, and he enclosed a five-shilling postal order. Coincidentally, the other letter from my Auntie Nora and Uncle Charlie also contained a five-shilling postal order. I was rich to the sum of ten shillings but as we didn't visit a post office, I brought them back home with me.

Mum must have cashed them and put the money into the household kitty because I don't recall spending them. However, it was good to have them in my possession for a few days.

At the end of the holiday, we were all bussed back and we said farewell to Rosebank Primary. After the summer break, we had a brand new school to look forward to. Or maybe not.

I expect the happy holidaymakers from Butlins all came back with glowing memories of swimming in the freezing cold outdoor pool, the dancing and the shows and all the fun and games organised by the Redcoats.

We came back with a smattering of nature, country living and red cheeks – in more ways than one – because someone was diagnosed with scarlet fever and we all arrived home clutching a letter warning our parents to look out for the warning signs of the disease. I never caught it and after a few weeks back in the grimy, smoky streets of Dundee, my complexion began to look less rosy.

Still, I was glad to be back home. There was time to play on the tops of the air raid shelters where gangs of kids would jump from one to the other, sending the people in the surrounding houses into a state of apoplexy. 'Eh've sent for the Bobby and he'll sort you lot oot,' said one woman, opening her window and hanging out, while shaking her fist at us.

Sometime this warning worked and we all skulked off but we were back the following evening, shouting and leaping like demented banshees.

Then we could also go to the Swannie Ponds to play. These ponds were actually called the Stobsmuir Ponds and during the war they were drained so that the water wouldn't be reflected in the moonlight, as this might alert the Luftwaffe.

At one time there had been little paddle boats for hire on the ponds but we never had the money to go on one. So we just ran around the edges of the water and played on the grassy banks.

On one visit, which I'm ashamed to remember, we all set off with my brother tagging along. As he was much younger than my pals and me, I was a bit miffed. But mum had said I had to take him so I had no choice.

I could see the accident happening before my eyes as he ran down the grassy slope that surrounded the edges of the ponds. He was running so fast he couldn't stop and he went straight into the water. Thankfully the water wasn't deep and he sank up to his waist and he soon scrambled out.

At that moment we were all having such fun with some game or other so I put him on the homeward-bound tram, soaking wet and cold.

Well, I got such an earful from Mum when I eventually scampered home. I tried to defend myself. 'Well eh pit him on the tramcar,' I said, like a midget version of Mother Teresa, all sweetness, light and sibling-caring. Mum was having none of these excuses. 'Well if he catches his death o cauld then it's your fault.'

Oh, the poor wee soul, to have such a rotten sister. Quite honestly I'm still amazed he still speaks to me.

As that summer wore on, the memory of Belmont Camp and my brush with country living began to fade, as did my rosy cheeks. Not like Butlins' Redcoats who went on for years afterwards, going about like chirpy Robin redbreasts, welcoming happy campers.

Still, I think the outdoor swimming pool at Butlins would have been just as freezing cold as the waters of the Swannie Ponds.

I must ask my brother how cold it was.

25

The Wild West Comes to Dundee

On 12 August 1904, the Wild West came to Dundee in the shape of Buffalo Bill's Wild West Show. It arrived at the Magdalen Green Park and set up its attractions. This show had been in Britain for almost two years and had visited 134 cities where it had played to rave revues.

And no wonder. There were 600 men and 500 horses, plus a stagecoach and real cowboys and genuine Red Indians. There was also horseback riding, shooting and big battles between the Indians and the cowboys.

How thrilling it must have been for the spectators to witness a real taste of the Wild West without leaving their hometown. Crowds turned out in their hundreds to see a real Indian Chief attack the stagecoach, and I bet it was pretty scary.

Buffalo Bill, always the showman, was also quite a character, dressed in the fashion of the frontier towns of America. It must have taken a lot of hard work and meticulous planning to bring this spectacle to Britain, especially as they toured all over the country. Transporting the people would have been not so difficult but I can't imagine how they managed to transport 500 horses and all the props like the stagecoach.

Remember this was away back in 1904 when there weren't the wide roads like today. The railways could have accommodated the people but did the horses also go by rail? And where did they put the Deadwood Stage?

Whatever, it was still a wonderful show that thrilled its audiences and I'm sure children must have been mesmerised by it all.

The era of the cowboy and Indian films lay in the future but the citizens of Dundee didn't need them. They had seen the real thing.

And before I'm pulled up for referring to the Native Americans as Red Indians, well that was what we always called them, before we knew any better, and were always yelling for the cavalry or the cowboys to beat them in battle. That was before we learned the history of these brave and noble people and how persecuted they were. Losing their lands to white settlers who didn't nurture the land like they did or protect the large herds of buffalo.

Yes, that's what we called them, away back in the dark days of yore.

When we didn't know any better.

26

Credit Crunch

Our street was divided down the middle about the thorny question of paying for goods. Quite a few of the households were proud of the fact that they never had any debt, always saving up diligently for any items needed in the house. My mother belonged to the other half that had to rely on getting essentials on tick. As she said, 'If we had tae save up for it, we wid never get it.'

The savers would say that by the time the items were paid for, it was time to get some more credit and therein lay the crunch. Still, being the sole bread-winner, Mum had no choice. The two main credit stores were McGills, at the top of the Wellgate steps, and the Star Stores in Constitution Road.

However, there was a third and better option, namely the 'Provie cheque'. Issued by the Provident Company, these cheques had the added benefit of being redeemable in various shops and the shoppers weren't restricted to one store.

Along with your cheque, you got a list of shops that

dealt with the company and the three I remember on the Hilltown were Sutherlands, L. S. Chalmers and a drapery and fancy goods shop on the corner of Alexander Street.

Mum always got the Provie man to issue a cheque at Christmas and maybe another two throughout the year. The problem was, although she had no qualms about getting them, she had an aversion to going out and spending them. 'Fowk will ken eh'm getting things on tick,' she would say, in the same tone she would use as if she had suddenly been discovered with her hand in the church poor box.

Personally, I couldn't have cared less what folk thought. We were paying for our goods just like everyone else, but it just took a wee bit longer. That was the main reason I was always sent with a list with the sizes and descriptions of things needed.

When clothes were on the ration, clothing coupons had to be produced with the cheque. When rationing was abolished, the shops were suddenly full of goods; food as well as clothing and domestic items. The customer now produced the cheque minus coupons and the only restriction was money. With a £2 or £3 cheque we had to watch the cost of things, whereas under rationing we were also restricted by how many coupons we had.

My favourite shop was L. S. Chalmers, which was a bright, modern shop with a couple of long counters with glass fronts. Behind this glass was a selection of nightdresses, pyjamas, socks, vests etc. It couldn't be compared to the supermarkets and stores of today with their thousands of stock items, but after the wartime austerity, the choices seemed enormous.

However, I had a sneaky liking for the shop on the corner of Alexander Street owned by Mr Rosen. It was an old-fashioned type of shop and I loved all the dark nooks and crannies, and the smell of varnished wood vying with the indefinable aroma of wool and new clothes.

On most of my excursions to the shops, I had to stand in a queue and wait to be served. Nothing was ever hurried. Drawers were pulled out and boxes opened while the customer made his or her choices but oh the delight when it was my turn to be served.

I studied my list. It was usually items of clothing for my brother and myself. 'Twa pairs of grey knee-length stockings, twa vests and one grey school shirt,' I said, rattling off the proper sizes and inspecting the goods that were laid out on the counter for my appraisal.

Once my purchases were made, the assistant would add up the cost, take the cheque and deduct the amount. The great thing about this credit facility was the fact that you could shop in any of the designated businesses until the full amount had been used up. I think Mum usually took out the sum of two pounds on a cheque.

One Christmas, I remember being sent off with my list. Mum had been a wee bit embarassed the previous Christmas when two of her pals had given us all a small present each. This year, Mum had added two gifts and my instructions were to buy something suitable. 'Eh'll leave it up to you tae get a wee thing for Nellie and Nan.'

I could barely wait to get into the shop. The elderly assistant brought out suitable gifts: embroidered handkerchiefs in small boxes of three; tea aprons; tea towels and crocheted doilies for the dressing table, which were also in sets of three. I was spoiled for choice and I can still recall the delicious indecision as I tried to make my mind up.

I settled for a flowery tea apron for Nellie and the hankies for Nan. Mum had also said to get a pair of school trousers for George for his Christmas and something for myself.

Before I set off, she warned me to make sure it was something sensible like another vest, but who wanted a boring old vest?

I decided to go to L. S. Chalmers for my gift. The entire shop was decked out for Christmas with stacks of perfumed coffrets with talcum powder, soap and wee bottles of scent. I immediately fell in love with one such coffret. It was the name that attracted me to it. It was called 'Attar of Roses'. I had no idea what 'attar' meant but it sounded exotic and held all the images of the inscrutable orient.

My wee box had talc and two bath cubes and smelled wonderful. Mum was pleased with most of the purchases but not with the Attar of Roses. 'Whaur are you ga'en tae use the bath cubes? In the kitchen sink?'

Oh, but I had no intention of using them. I wanted to keep the box in a drawer, only taking it out every so often to smell the perfume.

I had that box for years and it was only when we moved to our new house that I used the bath cubes. However, by then they were almost as fine as dust and the smell of roses had long vanished.

Over the years, I regularly did the 'Provie cheque shopping'. The items varied from year to year but I would choose something for Nan and Nellie every Christmas. They always looked delighted when opening their present. 'Och it's jist whit eh wanted Molly'. they would say. They never knew that Molly had no hand in buying the gifts.

Maybe they were being polite and really hated their gift but I somehow don't think so as their eyes always lit up. A sure sign of pleasure.

Nowadays, Christmas is a far grander time with expensive gifts and huge amounts of money being spent.

Like the credit cards of today, it all had to be paid back over the next few months but I'll never forget the joys of shopping with the Provident Company. Unlike a credit card, however, you could only spend your designated amount of money and this had to be paid back before another cheque was issued, which meant Mum could keep a strict eye on her spending.

One small thing. I never found another Attar of Roses box with talc and two bath cubes. Or a flowery tea apron. I know because I've looked. Not that I want to give them as a Christmas present to anyone. Except maybe myself.

27

Travels on a Tramcar

There were two pleasures when travelling on a tram. One was the actual journey and the second was the conversations overheard during the journey. I must admit that I loved listening to women chatting as they went into such intimate details.

'Do you mind o Ina wha used tae bide beside me? She was the sister of Bella wha used tae work in the Eagle Jute Mill. Well Ina took bad the other day and ch had tae send oot tae the chemist for a bottle of medicine.'

'Oh, eh mind o her. Did she used tae wear a wig?'

'No, you're thinking o Isa. She wore a wig for years because her hair fell oot on V. E. Day. It was seemingly the stress o the war thit did it. The doctor said she had alopecia or something like that.'

'Oh that must hiv been awfy, losing your hair like that. Did it ever grow back in again?'

'Eh've nae idea, eh hivnae seen her for donkey's years. No, this is Ina wha used tae gae to the same school as me. She's the big stoot wifie thit merried yon big lad, Bert. He wis ower six feet tall and she wis just a wee bauchle. But bonny wi it. Oh aye she wis a real bonnie lassie in her day.'

'Eh mind when Isa's wig blew aff.'

'Oh dinnie tell me. She must have been black affrontit wi the shame.'

'Oh aye, she was. We were pushing oor prams up tae the wash hoose one day and this muckle wind blew her hair tae one side. Eh tried no tae laugh but it wisnae easy.'

Sadly, this fascinating conversation came to an abrupt end when one of the women reached the end of her journey.

'Well here's my stop. It was nice seeing you again. Tell yer man, Tom, eh'm asking for him.'

After she disembarked, the other woman turned to another passenger behind her. 'My man's name's no Tom. Eh think she's getting me mixed up wi somebody else.'

Honestly, I tried also not to laugh but it wasn't easy.

Another bit of chit-chat happened soon after. Two old women who looked about eighty years old were having a great gossip about a wedding. The first woman was the narrator and she was dissecting the event, segment by segment.

'We wir at a wedding on Saturday. It was my man's cousin's sister-in-law's niece.' (At least I think that was the relationship but I could have remembered it wrong. It may have been her man's niece's sister-in-law's cousin but life's too short to work it out.)

'We didnae ken the couple and it was just a wee

affair. It wasnae a white wedding.' (At this statement there was a pregnant pause while I imagined the two women shared a look.) 'The bride was dressed in a grey frock.'

'My mother always said, "Get merried in grey, you'll rue the day,"' said her companion.

'Oh, eh've never heard that afore. Anyway it was a good day although it was pouring wi rain frae start tae finish. Then we went tae this wee hall up a pend for the reception. The meal was all right but the soup was a bit cauld, the biled ham was curled up at the edges and the pudding was jist a couple o mouthfuls o ice cream wi a wee daud o jelly.'

'That's a shame. It fair maks the wedding when you get a decent, substantial dinner.'

'The cup o tea wis nice and hot but the wedding cake was a bit stale eh thought.'

At this point I almost turned round and said that a great time was obviously had by all and I felt sorry for the poor bride in her 'rue the day' grey frock. However, the tale wasn't over.

'Did she get any wedding presents?'

'Dinnie mention that. We gave them a cruet set and whit dae you think? Did they no go and get another nine cruet sets. Still she also got five tea towels and three His and Her pillowslips.'

'Heavens, she was lucky.'

My sympathy for the bride increased tenfold – to match the ten cruet sets. Quite honestly I was annoyed when my stop came into view as it meant leaving behind all this wonderful insight into people's lives and I was tempted to stay on the tram, especially when the wedding saga was finished and she started on about her neighbour.

'Her doon the stairs frae me is a right auld nark. She keeps chapping up on her ceiling wi a brush if eh have the wireless on. The cheeky besom.'

He pal gave a loud snort of sympathy. 'Eh widnae put up wi that. Eh would gae doon tae her door and hammer on it then run back up the stairs again.'

Run back up the stairs? This couple were about eighty and here they were, acting like five year olds.

In the 1950s when launderettes were first established, these warm, soapy smelling places were also hotbeds of wonderful stories. Not only were they a blessing for households before washing machines became the norm, but the fact that the machine did all the hard work meant we all had time to laze around and gaze with fascination at the washing swirling around and listen to the latest gossip.

'Eh'm fair washed oot,' said one red-faced woman to her neighbour on the seat next to her.

The woman laughed. 'Oh that's a great joke. Fair washed oot in the launderette. Ha Ha Ha.'

'No, whit eh mean is this is my third visit here this morning. At this rate eh'll no have any mair room on my washing line and it'll mean eh've tae dry my claes in front o the fire and my man gets so annoyed when he has tae compete wi the wet washing tae get near the heat.'

Another woman butted in. 'You should put your washing in one o yon tumble dryers ower there.' She pointed in the direction of a large machine that was making whirring noises.

'But that costs mair money and as eh said, this is my third trip this morning. It's costing me a fortune. Eh could get my washing done at the wash hoose for a couple o bob instead of half a croon a go here.'

'But you would have tae work for it instead of sitting on your bum on this chair and letting the machine dae a the hard work,' said a young lass who looked as if she had never darkened the door of the wash house.

Years later when my two sons were sharing a flat in Dundee, they went every Saturday to the launderette at the top of the Hilltown. There had been a spate of burglaries and the focus of the conversation was on the dastardly deeds of the thieves; and as it turned out, not only thieves but picky thieves.

'Apparently they're no pinching videos. They tak everything else but leave the video ahent.'

'How dae you ken that?'

'Well my neighbour alang the street had a braw video recorder that she got for her silver wedding anniversary and the burglars didnae touch it. They took the telly and the wireless but no the video.'

'That's queer. Eh wonder why they leave them ahent?'

'Dinnie ken but they do.'

Perhaps the burglars realised that technology was moving on and DVDs and CDs were the new thing. There wouldn't be much sense in pinching old technology, would there?

This launderette was run by two very friendly women who liked to eat Pot Noodles at dinner time.

One day a young man came in carrying a gigantic rucksack on his back. He paid for one machine and began to empty his bag. It looked as if he had three months' washing and he proceeded to push it all into the machine. One sock dropped onto the floor and the two women and my son watched as he tried to push it in as well.

'Eh think you'll need a shoehorn, son,' said one woman, busy stirring her Pot Noodle. The man managed to squeeze it in, inch by inch and went to buy some soap powder.

'You'll need twa packets tae wash a that lot,' said woman number two. He then sat down and watched his clothes barely moving through the window. While everyone else's washing was birling merrily around, his was moving in a solid mass.

When the machine switched off, the lad could hardly unload his as the clothes had fused together in one huge lump which fell on the floor with a thud.

Everyone watched this drama and the two women nodded in triumph. 'Eh could hiv telt ye that ye needed three machines for your load, son. One machine wis nivver big enough.'

The lad however had done his washing and he wasn't caring if half of it was still unwashed. He packed up and left.

Two customers had watched all this fiasco and one turned to her companion. 'Eh thought that machine wis ga'en to explode.' Her pal nodded. 'Eh bet he's broken it and it nivver works again.'

On hearing this, the two custodians of the laun-derette scurried over and gave the machine a close inspection. All that was missing was the magnifying glass.

'Och if it ga'es on the blink we'll jist gie it a dunt and it should be okay.'

I was on a bus one day, just after a big football match between Dundee and Rangers that Dundee won by three goals to two. Two men were behind me.

'Grand game on Saturday, Bob.'

'Aye.'

'Great goal by Alfie Boyd.'

'Aye.'

'Were you at the match?'

'No.'

Oh for heaven's sake, I said to myself. What planet do men come from? It's certainly not Planet Chit-Chat. If it had been two wee wifies discussing the game, they would have described everything from the footballers' shorts, boots and haircuts to the state of the pitch and the weather. And they probably would have ripped to shreds any football fans within a ten mile radius, not to mention the hot pies and the luke-warm Bovril.

But I've left the best titbit till last. It wasn't a conversation, merely a snatch I overheard as I was leaving my bus.

'When she got hame frae her work her man was lying on the floor. What a shock she got.'

'Oh dinnie tell me he was dead.'

'Oh, he was dead all right. Dead drunk.'

28

A Family Story

There have been thousands of words written and films and documentaries made about World War I, or the Great War as it became known, but this is one man's own personal story.

I was five years old when my grandad, Charles Dwyer, died but such was the mark of the man that I have such vivid memories of him and I have to say that a lot of his philosophy on life has stayed with me.

I remember his stories and our trips, but he never mentioned the years that went before my knowing him.

Born in 1881, his parents died when he was three years old and, along with his brothers and sisters, he was sent to Smyllum Orphanage in Lanarkshire.

In 1897, he joined the Royal Garrison Artillery (Militia). Pretending he was eighteen years old instead of sixteen, he spent two and a half years with them before joining the Royal Dublin Fusiliers (RDF) with whom he served for thirteen years. I expect after years in an orphanage, the army must have seemed like a good idea to the young, auburn-haired boy, no doubt full of daring do and adventure not to mention the bed and board and uniform.

However, I am only surmising this reason. Perhaps he had a different agenda that I'll never know now.

His brother Andrew and cousin Charles were also with the RDF and two of his sisters went to work in Liff Hospital in 1897 so it looks as if they all left the orphanage around this time.

In 1914, my grandfather was still in the army but was now married to my grandmother, Fanny, and they had two children, Charlie and Molly. Being a widow before marrying grandad, she also had three children from her first marriage, Saunders, Jemima and Frances, who all lived with Fanny's parents. Sadly Jemima died in 1912 aged ten and Saunders died in 1920, aged twenty-one. Frances went on to marry and emigrated to Philadelphia. Fanny died in 1914 aged thirty-three. It must have been a huge tragedy in the family.

What a terrible time for grandad. He was now a widower with two small children, two stepchildren and a war was looming on the horizon.

When war broke out, the RDF, who were now part of the 10th brigade, 4th division, which then became part of the British Expeditionary Force (BEF), went to France almost immediately. The BEF were professional soldiers from the regular army and were known as the 'Old Contemptibles' or in the case of the 2nd Battalion Dublin Fusiliers 'The Old Toughs'.

During the retreat from Mons, which was their first battle, they delayed the German Army's march to

Paris. They caused such heavy casualties that the Germans thought they were facing a barrage of machine guns when in fact each battalion had only two machine guns. It was the riflemen who provided this rapid-fire cover.

Then it was on to the second battle of Ypres, or Wipers as the soldiers called it. The 2nd Dublins took part in all but one of the battles that took place between 22 April and 24 May 1915.

The first day of the battle on 22 April was marked by the first use of chlorine gas by the German Army and on 23 April, the 2nd Battalion was rushed forward to stem the German breakthrough. In the mud and gore of the trenches at the battle of St Julien they suffered hundreds of casualties. On 24 April the Germans released a second cloud of chlorine gas. Directly in line with the spread of the deadly gas were Canadian soldiers stationed to the west of the village of St Julien. On seeing the gas approach the trenches, word went round for the troops to urinate on their handkerchiefs and place them over their mouths and noses. This was an ineffective measure and the Germans pushed through the lines to capture the village.

Grandad survived these battles. The following two battles at Frezenberg and Bellewaarde would see further carnage and on 24 May they were sent into line at Mouse Trap Farm where they faced a major gas attack. Out of a total of 668 men, 647 became casualties of gas poisoning.

During the period 25 April to 25 May, 127 men were killed and 1,094 were posted as missing.

The war was over for grandad and most of his comrades. He was shipped home on the hospital ship *Valdivia* and was treated at the Bagthorpe Hospital in Nottinghamshire.

Although he didn't know it then, his health would never be the same again. His damaged lungs would never heal and he died in 1943 aged sixty-three.

However, that was all in the future and in 1916 he re-enlisted in the Royal Garrison Artillery, then in 1918 joined the Royal Engineers until finally being discharged from the army at Chatham in 1919.

No words can describe the horrors and deprivation of trench warfare and the horrendous number of young men's deaths; some of them still in their teens.

At the start of the war, thousands of men rushed to join up in a fervour of patriotism and Dundee was no exception. Lord Kitchener had devised the idea of the 'New Armies' but the men weren't fully trained. The city raised its own battalion, which was affectionately known as 'Dundee's Ain'.

During the battles of Neuve Chapelle and Loos it was said that every second home in Dundee received a telegram from the War Office with news of the death of a loved one. And in some cases more than one because sometimes brothers were killed, either together or in separate battles. As were groups of pals who had all joined up together.

It must have been a terrible time of mourning in the city. I can't even begin to comprehend the destruction to entire families with the grief and loss.

On 16 May 1925, the dedication of the new war memorial on top of the Law Hill took place. The memorial was unveiled by General Sir Ian Hamilton who paid testament to the 4,050 men who were killed in battle in an eloquent speech.

The luminous mass of Cornish granite breaks free from the Imperial colours in which it was swathed and stands four-square upon the Law Hill where there is no reason why it should not endure till the scientists who invented poison gas carry out their principles to a logical conclusion and explode their own planet.

He then paid tribute to the fallen, saying:

Off they went singing 'And it's Ho! for the West Port and let us gae free.' And westwards they went and down went 'the bonnets o Bonnie Dundee.'

That wonderful legend of theirs will ever be linked to the fame of the Black Watch. This regiment of high renown. With valiant fighters suffering for that fame. Pushed time after time, wounds still bleeding, into the forefront of the hottest battles.

Sir Ian went on to express his dismay at the distress faced by the families of the soldiers who had died and the men who had returned from war:

Many of the comrades of the dead still exist more dead than alive on the dole and it is the duty of the State to think of the stomachs as well as the souls of its old soldiers and to start work of national importance.

Sentries stood at each corner of the base resting on reversed arms. They were selected from units of the Royal Naval Volunteer Reserve (RNVR), 4th/5th Black Watch, 76th (Highland) Field Brigade RA and 237th Field Company Royal Engineers.

Representatives from the services were lined up

along with limbless soldiers and the aged and infirm members of the families of the fallen men. The Guard of Honour was the 4th/5th Black Watch under the command of Captain Douglas Urquhart. In front of the guard stood Lieutenant Kirkcaldy bearing the colour of the regiment. The RNVR brass band and the 4th/5th Black Watch pipe band stood close to the memorial.

There were also representatives from the Girl Guides, the Girls Guildry, the Scouts and The Boys Brigade. Two schoolchildren, Alex Smith and Bella Old, laid a wreath on behalf of the city's schoolchildren.

After the service of dedication was over, the members of the public were then lined up and they made their way to the top of the hill to pay their respects to the dead. The majority of them would have been parents, wives, sweethearts, brothers and sisters who wanted to commemorate the sad occasion in their own way.

I've no idea if my grandad was one of those mourners but knowing him as I do, I'm almost certain he would have been in that line, to pay homage to his fallen comrades who never made it home.

If it is said quickly, 4,050 doesn't sound a lot and we can never fully comprehend the scale. It is just a number, but for anyone wanting to realise the true carnage of war then go to the local library and read the *People's Journal* dated 16 and 25 May 1925 to see the photos of all the young men who died. Look into their eyes and weep.

The war went on for another three years after

grandad was repatriated and there were many more horrendous battles like the Somme, Passchendaele and Gallipoli and thousands more deaths.

The Somme (Don't Think)
The officer shouted, 'Over the top.'
Pick up your heels, run till you drop.
Don't think about your loving wife,
Or the children who are the light of your life.
Forget the girl who kissed you goodbye,
Who vowed to be true as time went by.
Never mind that your life has been in vain,
That you'll never see your home again.
Don't think about the tears and pain,
Or lying dead in the pouring rain.

Another shameful part of the war was the dawn executions of soldiers who were deemed to have deserted. Young lads, who suffered from shell shock or from the stress of all the death and gore, were given no measure and were shot at dawn as deserters. Their families never knew what happened to their sons, husbands or fathers as their deaths were simply stated as missing, believed dead.

Dawn Execution
The shell exploded with a terrible noise,
Hurting his eyes and shattering his ears.
His comrades lay dead, they were only boys,
While he survived with a heart full of fear.

Lying in the putrid mud,
Surrounded by a dreadful stench
Of broken men who spilled their blood
In this God-forsaken trench,

His thoughts went back to a peaceful life
With his loving wife and baby sons.
Then the whistle blew, it was time for strife,
To run into the battle and the blasting guns.

The officers wouldn't accept his plea.
Although his spirit was willing, his legs had gone
So they lined him up against a tree
And shot him in the grey light of dawn.

After the war, grandad and thousands like him faced another battle, namely unemployment as the Great Depression took hold.

In General Hamilton's speech he said not to forget the sacrifice of the old soldiers and that the State should make sure they were properly housed, fed and employed.

Of course the State did no such thing. The men who had fought and sacrificed themselves for King and Country were now embarrassments. The government let men languish on the dole. Entire families were starving and rioting took place on the streets of Dundee.

It was a terrible first quarter of the new century.

As for the rest of the speech, well it did come true and the world still has its wars and people blowing other human beings to bits and other such horrors as poison gas in one form or another. Maybe now called a different name but still as lethal. In Britain, brave soldiers are dying in places like Iraq and Afghanistan and it seems like nothing changes.

I was lucky. Grandad survived until 1943, just long enough for me to get to know him. If it wasn't for my cousins, Carolyn and Pam, in particular, who have researched the family tree, I would never have known about his life before I knew him and what a life he led. A true soldier who never mentioned any of his exploits. Nor did he become bitter about life.

Grandad had seven grandchildren and as the oldest I am the only one who remembers him. I recall he was a quiet, gentle man, a true peacemaker who loved to knit and was a good cook. I am truly grateful to have had this insight into his early life, thanks to the painstaking work done by the Dwyer family. They have has brought him to life. A life we knew nothing about till now.

One thing did change however. The Great War was the last conflict where young men and women went into battle with a romanticised feeling of adventure and patriotism. It was all going to be over by Christmas they were told.

For thousands of men, it was.

Ypres
It must have been a terrible day:
The mud and rain, the cries of pain;
The mustard yellow chlorine gas that would ooze and seep
Into men's lungs and eyes,
To make them weep
At Wipers.

It must have been a hellish sight
For the Dubliners,
And Charles Dwyer who went to fight
For King and Country,
To set things right
at Wipers.

This former placid grassy plain
Was turned into a bloody chaotic place,
For thousands of men
Who perished
In the mud and rain
At Wipers.

Although Charles Dwyer survived the fight,
Only God knows why
He lived to see another night.
But when he died in 1943
His body merely joined his spirit left behind at the site
    of Wipers.

29

Calling a Spade a Spade

The world is now obsessed with political correctness.
No more calling a chairman by that gender or a
cleaner by that lowly name. Now it's some high faluting
title like 'Hygiene Operative'.

I know that a lot of derogatory words are now
consigned to history's bin and quite rightly so, but
things have gone a bit over the top these days.

I sometimes wonder how my mum would have
coped with all the new rules. Not that she would ever
be rude to anyone, or racist, but her sense of humour,
I think, would have got her into trouble with the heid
yins.

She was in the post office one afternoon, the one at
the top of the Hilltown where she was a well-known
customer. Lying on the floor was a child's plastic gun
that some kiddie had dropped. She picked it up and
pointed it at the woman behind the counter. 'Put your
hands up, this is a stick up,' she said, in her best James
Cagney voice.

The woman assistant roared with laughter. 'Och

that'd the best laugh eh've had a' day. You've forgot tae put on yer mask, Molly. Eh'll be able tae pick you oot in a police line-up.'

At that moment, much to my embarrassed relief, the small owner of the gun came in with his mum. He was dressed in a cowboy outfit with a little suedette waistcoat, trousers, a hat and an empty holster.

'Oh you've found Bobby's gun, thank goodness,' said his mum.

'Eh'm jist keeping this baddie from raiding the cattle ranch, cowboy,' said Mum to the wee boy who didn't have a clue what she was talking about.

Personally, I was glad to escape from the shop but the assistant was still laughing and telling all her customers what had happened.

Of course, Mum had learned all this American jargon from reading her *True Crime* magazines which she bought in Marshalls, the second-hand book shop on the Hilltown, or from reading her detective novels from the library.

We went to the library in Albert Square at least three times a week. While I liked to roam all over the building and look at some of the more serious books, I don't think Mum ever went anywhere but the thriller section. Still it has to be said that this was the busiest section in the entire library.

I mean, there was I, all alone in the aisle reading a book on world travel while half the population of Dundee was crowded around the shelves of the thrillers. There was always a gasp of anticipation when the librarian came to put new books on the shelves and I personally thought it was a bit of a scramble.

'Oh, eh just love the Crime Club books,' said one woman to her companion. 'If you see the Crime Club sign you ken it's going tae be a good read.'

Mum just loved anything. Agatha Christie, Raymond Chandler or any book with dead bodies.

Mind you, I'm just pretending to be intellectual as I always read the thrillers as well and enjoyed them. It was a bit of escapism.

There used to be a newspaper called the *Reveille* and one of its running stories was about one of their reporters who went around the country. The paper would announce in advance which city he would visit and they offered a money prize to anyone who recognized him.

He would stand on a street with a *Reveille* under his arm and the paper said that anyone who knew him had to say a special phrase and they would get the money.

Every week, the paper was full of happy and delighted winners all gazing with beaming smiles at the camera and holding up their prize.

Mum loved this story and one week it was announced that the man was coming to Dundee. 'Oh, we'll have tae look oot for him,' she said. Over my dead body I thought.

As luck would have it, we were coming out of Gray's the bakers, who had a shop at the top of the Hill, when we saw a man standing at the foot of Hill Street. He was trying to look nonchalant and he had a newspaper under his arm.

Mum was ecstatic. She poked me in the ribs and said, 'It's that man frae the *Reveille*.'

I almost died because I knew what was coming next.

'Now Maureen, jist you gae ower and say you want the prize.' There was just one wee problem to this plan. She couldn't remember the exact phrase and that was one of the conditions of winning. The words had to be right and as printed in the paper.

She had a few shots at it. 'You're the man frae *Reveille* and I claim my prize. No that's no it. I claim my prize because I recognize you. No that's no right.' She turned to me.

'Can you no mind the exact words?'

I shook my head. 'No Mum.'

She gave me a look that said I was some sort of backward idiot. 'Well eh thought you would mind what tae sae. You've aye got an answer for everything else.'

She gave another glance at the man but no one else seemed to notice him.

'We'll have tae hurry up or he'll go awa tae some other street.'

I hoped and prayed that he would but he seemed to be glued to the spot.

'I think you have tae say, "You're the man frae *Reveille* and I am claiming my prize." I'm sure that's right. Now awa you go ower and say that.'

'Mum he might no be the man frae *Reveille*.'

'Eh'm sure he is. He's standing there looking awfy suspicious like, and eh bet he's jist waiting on somebody going ower and claiming the prize.' This statement was delivered with another dig in the ribs. 'Jist go ower, he'll no eat you.'

Well I never thought he would, as he looked so innocuous as he stared into space.

'He might be waiting for his wife tae come oot o Johnstone's Stores,' I said, more in hope than anything.

'Well why is he standing at the foot of Hill Street if he's waiting on his wife? If he was waiting for somebody he would be standing outside the shop.'

I couldn't argue with that so to keep her quiet, I rehearsed my words and wandered over, hoping no one I knew was in the vicinity.

As I approached him, the man looked at me. 'You're the man from *Reveille* and I claim my prize,' I said, trying hard not to stutter, my face as red as a beetroot.

He burst out laughing. 'I wish I was, hen.'

I went back to Mum and was I furious. 'He's no the man frae *Reveille* and you hivnae got any prize,' I said through clenched teeth.

'You must have said the words wrong,' she said, disbelief written all over her face. 'Eh wish eh could remember them.'

Much to my relief she walked away but still looking backwards, no doubt looking to see if someone else approached him but he stood there like a statue, looking as nonchalant as an Eskimo in the Sahara.

She couldn't wait to get the paper the following week. Seemingly the prize was won by someone outside McGills shop on the Wellgate steps.

'Och that's where he was,' she said, disappointment sounding in every word. Then she brightened up. 'Eh still say that was him but you got the words wrong.'

So it was my fault.

She was also full of little dire warnings about dirty ears and other personal idiosyncrasies. It was just as well I didn't believe her when she said potatoes grew out of dirty ears otherwise I would have had nightmares.

Although mortified at the time by her humour, I can now look back with affection. Mum didn't have a lot in life to be cheery about but we did get lots of laughs.

No doubt in this politically-correct world she wouldn't get off with larking about with a child's plastic gun or encouraging her daughter to approach a total stranger but we lived in a more innocent time when you could call a spade a spade without calling it a garden, flat-bladed implement.

Motherspeak
Do you remember, Mother?
Those far-off days of childhood,
When you told me potatoes grew out of dirty ears?
How I scanned the mirror for months afterwards.
Watching and waiting.
Scared stiff I would emerge as the star of some
   Hollywood horror film.
When I squinted in the bright sunshine
You warned me that should the wind change course,
I would turn into a perpetually, demented, grimacing
   gargoyle.
The wet, unboiled face flannel
Was another watchword in life's dictionary.
Its slimy surface harbouring a multitude of unspeakable
   horrors.
Do you remember, Mum?
The far-off days of Motherspeak?
Those wonderful golden nuggets of nonsense
So precious to me now you are on the verge of leaving
   me.

30

A Close Shave

We passed a barber's shop the other day and there was a price list in the window. A basic haircut was £8, which is the going rate these days, according to my husband.

We then went on to the supermarket which was the size of Dens Park and pushing a trolley around this vast cavern took ages, especially when looking for something small. I searched high and low for a deodorant but still couldn't find one. I looked in the right aisle and although there were twenty different toothpastes and scores of shampoos, conditioners and various forms of hair gels, the elusive deodorant was hiding from view.

I felt exhausted when leaving, a feeling that was made worse by the fact we only went in for two items and came out with three bags full and a till receipt for £81.45. How do they do it? Is there a form of hypnotism at the front door that makes customers suddenly desire three bags full like Baa Baa Black Sheep?

It made me think back to the old days when there

were just the little shops to buy from. Usually owned by one man or woman who seemed to make a decent living out of their little business, you went in with a list, which they ran around getting for you. You didn't get seduced into purchasing twenty-four toilet rolls in order to get two free, or a mega packet of soap powder that needs a crane to carry it out of the door and a 4x4 car to get it home.

One shop I remember with affection was Lottie Henderson's paper shop on the Hilltown. A tiny shop by any standard, it was made even more miniscule by the piles of newspapers on the counter. In fact, it was often impossible to see Lottie. Her technique however was spot on.

No matter what paper you asked for, she immediately found it and slapped it down on the top of the pile. Getting the money to her was a bit of a problem, especially when I was a child as it would have needed a small stepladder to reach her hands.

The fruiterer in Ann Street was another one-woman business. Potatoes were kept in a wooden-type bunker with a small trapdoor at the front and she would use a shovel to scoop them up and throw them on the scale. Cutting a turnip was hair-raising as she kept a large knife – or maybe it was a machete – nearby and she would hit the turnip with it, giving it an almighty thump and neatly slicing it in half.

There was also a selection of barbershops on the Hilltown and, unlike the modern shop of today with all its big mirrors and upholstered chairs, the shops of yesteryear were plain affairs.

The windows nearly all held a few sun-bleached

cardboard adverts for Brylcreem and small colonies of dead flies.

Inside was just as spartan with perhaps a couple of kitchen chairs and a pile of *Hotspur* and *Commando* comics, all well-thumbed with some of the pages missing.

One occasion I'll never forget took place in the 1960s. For some reason none of the male members of the family had had a haircut for months and they all had that shaggy look. So one Saturday afternoon we all trooped into Louis Lumsden's barbershop that lay directly across from Shepherd's Pend and plonked ourselves down on the row of empty chairs.

The reason we chose this barber above everyone else was the fact his shop was empty, which meant there would be no waiting and we could be in and out quickly. I wish.

The three boys pounced on the comics while their dad got his hair cut first. The barber, a cheery man, started off with bright chatter, about football and the sorry state of the world.

At that point, I'm sure he thought he just had the one customer and we were all waiting for him. He soon realised how wrong that assumption was.

It was now time for son number one whose hair had sprouted like a gigantic haystack. The brave barber tackled it manfully but kept glancing over at the other two boys who looked like wild men from Borneo.

Half an hour later it was time for son number two whose hair was slightly less thick than the other two but it still took another half hour to get into shape.

Son number three then made his way to the chair and I'm sure I heard a muffled groan coming from the poor man.

At that point, he turned to where I was sitting with my daughter. Wendy was clutching a tattered *Commando* book in her little fists and gazing intently at all the mayhem portrayed on the pages.

'Are you twa needing your hair cut as weel?'

I said no, we were just waiting.

The relief on his face was comical and I felt really sorry for him. The fact that it was a hot summer day didn't help, as the shop was stifling.

'When did you lot last get yer hair cut?' he asked. 'Was it afore the last war?'

Very funny.

Two and a half hours later we all emerged into the sunlight with the three boys and their Dad looking like shorn sheep.

Leaving behind the shop floor covered in enough hair to fill a mattress and with the huge sum of six shillings and threepence for all his hard work. That worked out at half a crown for my husband and one and threepence for each child. Now, for all the people born after 1971, that is equivalent to about thirty-two pence.

In my opinion, decimalisation put the cost of living up by nearly one hundred per cent. There were 240 pennies to the old pound and the new pound has 100 pennies. So something that cost eleven pennies in old money, which was a penny short of a shilling, went up overnight to eleven new pence, which was over two shillings. It was all down to the magic word, 'new' pence. We all thought we were still dealing in pennies. But we weren't.

But I digress. Back on the barber theme, we never went back to his shop as I'm sure he would have locked up and emigrated at the first sight of us.

A few years later, while staying with their grand-parents, Alick, George and Steven were taken to the barber by their grandad. Their hair was cut to within an inch of their life and the barber used the hand clippers to cut any stray tufts that escaped his scissors. In fact, it looked as if they didn't have any hair, just dirty scalps.

I almost cried when I saw them. They looked like escapees from Alcatraz and it crossed my mind that this was the same barber we had visited a couple of years before. If it was, he was making sure it would be a couple of years before they would be back.

I gave a mental count when faced with the modern barber's list and worked out it would now cost a family of four well over twenty pounds for the job. And then I remembered why, all those years ago, the men in the family had such long hair. It was because I had to save up the six shillings and threepence.

So everything is relevant to its own time.

31

The Bermuda Triangle

I once owned a handbag. It was advertised as an organiser bag, which was a bit of a misnomer to begin with because it was the most disorganised item I had. Apart from that, I was convinced this bag harboured a Bermuda Triangle in its depths.

Things kept disappearing and I once lost the electricity and telephone bills in its dark interior, never to return again. I don't remember how I paid these bills but as nothing was ever cut off, I must have managed somehow.

I was also the woman about whom 'Irate Man' wrote to the letters page of the newspaper;

Dear Sir

I was behind this idiotic woman in the shop the other day and it took five minutes for the checkout girl to ring through her groceries and another half hour while she rummaged in her bag for her purse/chequebook/card.

Yours truly
Irate Man.

I almost replied that I was organised and had the bag to prove it and wanted to explain it wasn't me but the fault of the Bermuda Triangle but I don't think he would have believed me. Quite honestly I couldn't believe it myself.

What was worse was the fact the Bermuda Triangle syndrome had also moved to the house and items disappeared on a regular basis only to reappear later.

The biro pens were the first. I bought a large pack of twenty pens and within two days they had all disappeared. I searched high and low but no sign of them. Then ten days later I found the entire twenty huddled together in the kitchen. They looked as if they had all arrived en masse from some biro pen convention and were now comparing notes.

Then there were the disappearing drawing pins. As soon as the Christmas decorations and cards came down at Epiphany, the pins were all carefully placed in a wee box with a picture of themselves on the front. So far so good, until one was needed and I discovered they had vanished – box and all. As with the pens, they all appeared out of the blue one summer day and I can only surmise they had rented themselves out to another house; a house with teenage bedrooms and numerous posters to be hung on the wall no doubt.

I keep the tape measure tightly rolled up on a shelf where it seems happy enough until I need it. Then off it goes walkabout for weeks before coming back home. When it returns it is all coiled up and wearing a smug expression. Perhaps it's been on its holiday where it spent a sun-soaked month inching its way across some golden beach in Majorca.

The worst disappearance, however, is of the scissors. They are a large, black-handled pair that hang from a hook in the kitchen and are quite content to dangle there until urgently required, especially when cooking the tea, courtesy of Birds Eye Boil-in-the-Bag. Everything is bubbling and boiling away and the scissors are not there.

Now, I draw the line at attacking the boil bag with my teeth and after umpteen tries with a sharp knife, I'm left with gravy and bits of meat all over the breadboard, the potatoes are cold and the peas have given up and died. Later, I find the scissors in the bread bin where they lurk as if in the huff.

In the future, should anyone excavate our house, they will find a multitude of pens, drawing pins, tape measures and scissors, plus many other things that go missing in the dead of night.

Will these learned people all nod wisely to themselves, saying they have found the real Bermuda Triangle?

It's not near the Bahamas after all but right here Chez Reynolds.

32

On Yer Bike

After we left Dundee and went rural, I became the proud owner of a smashing yellow Yamaha moped with a matching yellow helmet.

My workmates called me Penelope Pitstop from *Whacky Races*, except for one lone voice who would mutter something about the Yellow Peril.

About this time, a certain Norman Tebbit was urging everyone to 'Get on yer Bike' and go and look for work but I had beaten him to it by a few months.

I loved my bike and felt I had the freedom of the roads and the wind in my face and all that romantic rubbish. If I imagined the open road to be free from obstacles then I was soon put right on that matter.

Sunday mornings were always the wildlife journeys. There were the hedgehogs with a death wish, kamikaze rabbits, crows that dined alfresco in the middle of the road and pheasants that forgot they owned wings and would always do a runner in front of me, often getting their wings clipped in the process.

Loitering sheep were another menace. They would lurk on corners, just waiting to stroll nonchalantly in front of any motorist or biker stupid enough to be in their territory. Or else, sleep in the middle of the road and refuse to budge until nudged by the motorist. They would then trot off only to turn sharply and trot back from whence they came.

Then there were the deer. One memorable morning, I was joined by a small roe deer that resembled Bambi. For some unknown reason it decided to race along beside me and I could hear its hooves clattering on the tarmac. I looked in my mirror for Thumper but he must still have been playing somewhere else. Frightened in case I injured Bambi, I gave up and stopped. As it bounded away into the bracken, it gave me a 'What a Wimp and Spoilsport' look. I felt rotten for the rest of the journey. It isn't every day you see a playful deer that looks like Bambi.

Two days later I met its dad. A huge stag with gigantic antlers jumped over a wall and landed on the road a few feet from me. I don't know who got the bigger fright but he gave me a hostile glare, no doubt wondering what kind of yellow animal had dared to challenge him. After a heart-stopping moment he dismissed my threat and leapt over another wall and disappeared into the distance. I kept thinking all the way home that had I set off on my journey a few seconds earlier, the stag would have landed squarely on me and my bike. I imagined the headline in the local paper. 'Woman and moped squashed by stag.'

Man-made obstacles were also a nuisance; road

chippings in particular. Signs were always placed stating twenty miles an hour but that didn't stop boy racers and often grandad racers from flying along and scattering stone chips in every direction including my helmet, which soon had a sandblasted effect.

The bike didn't like this new road surface either and often went into a series of skids, twists and pirouettes that would have made Rudolf Nureyev proud and sorted out the bike riders from the rest of humanity.

Springtime could be the cruellest time. One moment warm sunshine and the next cold icy showers that dripped down your neck while icy winds left my hands numb until three o'clock in the afternoon.

Winged insects also played their part in the rich tapestry of life on the road. I was driving along one summer's evening, minding my own business when a bumble bee flew underneath my visor. Trying to concentrate on the road while Mr Bee played Rimsky-Korsakov on drums was impossible, so I jumped off the bike and stood on the roadside doing the Hokey Cokey. Shaking my helmet, 'In out, in out, shake it all about.'

However, the worst culprits of all were the midgies; those miniscule black specks of devilment. In my opinion, Scotland doesn't need a nuclear deterrent. Any invader foolhardy enough to try and subdue us during a wet summer would surely be driven insane by these insects, and their armies would head off for the sea and probably swim towards wherever they came from.

When meeting a black cloud of midgies, I always

put on my grim 'Don't mess with me' face but one night I accidentally swallowed one.

What a dilemma. Should I stand at the roadside and try to be sick or manfully soldier on and try to forget the whole horrendous episode? I did the latter, telling myself that in some countries a midgie might be looked upon as a source of protein, costing four pounds fifty a punnet to boot.

Long after Mr Tebbit disappeared from the political scene, I was still biking up and down the roads. At 120 miles to the gallon of petrol it was a cheap version of travel.

Terms like global warming, climate change and carbon footprints lay in the far distant future but with hindsight I like to think I was doing my bit for the planet.

It also kept the wildlife population guessing about the Yellow Peril in their midst.

33

Easter Parade

Easter Sunday was a special treat during the Spring holiday and there was always great anticipation a few weeks in advance of the day.

The reason for this feeling was the 'egg-rolling day' at the Den O'Mains; a trip that saw scores of people make there way to this leafy, grassy and extremely scenic spot, situated not far from the busy Kingsway.

In our house, preparations for this event normally started early in the day with the boiling of two eggs. For some reason, Mum never seemed to buy brown eggs. Ours were always snowy white and to give them some colour we would boil them in a solution of weak tea.

After ten minutes in this solution they emerged with a nice healthy tan, almost as if they had been sunning themselves on the beach. Then, after they cooled down, it was time to paint them. I had a small painting set which was a tinplate box filled with eight small squares of paint and a threadbare brush that sported six or seven bristles.

Still that didn't dampen our enthusiasm and George and I would take turns to paint faces on our eggs. This was a bit of a hit-or-miss venture as the paint kept sliding off the smooth eggshells, but we weren't too fussed about that. As long as we had a semblance of some features we were happy.

Then it was time to make our way to roll our eggs. I can't recall ever getting any sort of transport to the Den O' Mains and I'm sure we always walked all the way, along with half the population of Dundee.

When we reached our destination, it was always a scramble to get a nice spot to sit. There were prams with babies and toddlers in pushchairs, plus all the children running about shouting while mums and dads tried to settle everyone down. Sometimes entire extended families would all be grouped around the blankets: grannies, grandads, uncles, aunties and numerous children. It was a hard job trying to get a small piece of grass but this just added to the festive air.

Some families took along picnics, the mother emptying her large message bag which seemed to be filled to capacity with sandwiches, biscuits, tea and the hard-boiled eggs.

I don't think we ever saw one chocolate Easter egg in all the years we went egg-rolling.

George and I would try and sit near the grassy slope that was the venue for the egg-rolling and we would settle down with our picnic. We always travelled light; a paper bag with two jam pieces and the two eggs.

After scoffing our sandwiches, we would run up the

slope along with a horde of children and roll our eggs down to the bottom. As there were scores of similar eggs, it was sometimes difficult to find your own but that is where the dodgy painted faces came into their own.

Not many children had one eye at the front of the egg and the other at the back. George and I were truly in the Salvador Dali school of art with our unrealistic faces and it paid off when we spotted our strange creations lying forlornly in the thick grass.

After a few runs up and down the slope, it was now time to crack the shells and eat our eggs. Sometimes the egg was covered with grass and bits of twigs but a quick wipe over with your hand soon sorted that out.

After our picnic was eaten we would content ourselves by watching everyone else eat theirs. I lived in hope that someone would toss us a biscuit or another jammy piece but it never happened. I expect people just had enough food for their own families and there was never anything left over.

We would then run up the slope and launch ourselves downwards, rolling like the eggs until coming to a sharp bump at the foot. Sometimes you had to wait in a queue to get a chance to do this as most, but not all, of the children enjoyed this caper.

Looking back, I would like to imagine that these Easter Sundays were always sun-filled and warm, when we could stretch out on the grass and soak up the sunshine but I have to be honest and say that days like that were few.

I can remember it being so cold that everyone was muffled up with thick coats, scarves and gloves. Or else it was wet and the grass was damp. Some people with foresight came armed with an old army blanket that they spread over the wet grass but we relied only on our coats, which soon became wet and cold and uncomfortable to wear.

Still the weather might have dampened our coats but never our spirit.

We did learn about the biblical story of Jesus and the Crucifixion and sang with great gusto, a particular favourite hymn of mine 'There is a Green Hill Far Away'.

However, the symbolic rolling of eggs was lost on George and I and we never associated it with the stone rolling away from the tomb of Jesus. We just thought it was a fun thing to do.

It was a great day out in the fresh air, albeit a cold or wet one and I'm sure I recall some snowy times, but it cost very little and as we made our way back home in the late afternoon, we were tired out and starving.

Do children of today ever roll hard-boiled eggs down a grassy slope? If they do, I bet they don't eat them afterwards and who can blame them, what with all the litter and pollution around.

One Easter, a few years ago, a young acquaintance of mine stated proudly that she had received fourteen chocolate eggs, all of them filled with a selection of different sweeties. 'I'm not going to eat them all at once,' she said, sounding virtuous like Mother Teresa. 'I'm going to have one a day.'

I should jolly well think so, I thought. The younger generation have made this gigantic leap from the wartime years and beyond: from a world of food scarcity to a world where everything under the sun is stacked up high in the shops; we've moved away from little thin bars of 'Five Boys' chocolate to gigantic slabs that weigh a ton and measure twelve inches by ten inches.

I read about some school that did a lesson once on living during wartime. The children were all asked how they thought they would cope with going into a shelter when the siren went off.

The answers were funny. One boy thought there was nothing to it. 'I'll take some packets of crisps, apples, bananas and bars of chocolate to eat,' he said.

Another, when asked how he would entertain himself said, 'I'll take my iPod and X-Box player with my computer games, my mobile phone, and maybe Mum will put in the television and computer.'

The teacher told them there weren't all those things back then. That there was no electricity in the shelters nor packets of crisps, bananas and chocolate. Nor televisions, iPods and computers.

The kids were gobsmacked. They couldn't visualise a world without all its modern gadgets.

What I could have told them was that they could have had a jammy piece and a hard-boiled egg decorated with a strange face and covered in grass.

But I didn't.

34

And Finally

I've always wanted to be a writer, except for a very short time away back in 1952. We were all in Miss Calvert's English class and explaining what we would like to do after leaving school. I can't remember how many classmates spoke before me but when it was my turn, I stood up and said I wanted to be a mannequin.

As with all the others before me, the teacher threw the occupations open to the class for discussion while giving her own opinion on our choices. When I had finished giving my spiel, Miss Calvert said she didn't think a mannequin's career was suitable for me and she asked the class, 'Now why don't you think Maureen would make a good mannequin?'

One hand shot up. 'Because mannequins have to be pretty.' Thank you dear classmate of 1AMC. All I can say to her, is, 'May the moose *aye* leave yer girnal wi a tear in its e'e.'

Now the teacher said this wasn't the reason and I was pretty. Well teachers have to say these things don't they? After all, they are supposed to fill their pupils with confidence, otherwise we'll never believe another word they say.

No, what she meant was I wasn't quiet enough, being quite a lippy person at the time.

At that point it was time for plan B and to tell the class I wanted to be an authoress. In those dark days of sex discrimination, every male job that was coveted by a female always ended in -ess, as in poetess etc. Thankfully, all that nonsense has disappeared.

I recall being quite serious as I explained what tools I would need for this mythical job. 'A lot of paper and pencils,' I said, without a blush on my face. If only it had been as easy as that. With hindsight I would have stood a better chance of success if I had put my name down for the first moon trip. But of course that was all in the future.

I was nudging fifty when I seriously gave writing another thought and this eureka moment in my life coincided with the purchase of a second-hand typewriter.

This machine was perfect except for one little fault, as the woman who gave it to me explained, handing over a minute piece of plastic that was seemingly a broken bit that could be replaced.

Needless to say I never did get the replacement, which meant I had to insert the paper in the machine sideways and do a lot of jiggling around to square it up. This was fine when writing small articles but would have been time-consuming while writing my grand 'Meaning of Life' novel.

Undaunted, I entered a short story contest. Later,

along with the letter saying I hadn't won, was a card inviting me to join a writing school.

Although I never thought I would win I was still a bit disappointed when told I hadn't won, so I didn't keep the card.

A few weeks later I received another card saying if I didn't reply immediately, my name would be taken off their books. Well no one wants to be wiped from the great world of literary brilliance, but as the course cost quite a bit of money that I didn't have, I wasn't tempted.

I was now entering the harsh world of the publishing houses and it seemed to be a case of too many writers chasing too few publishers and it was a case of 'Don't call us. We'll call you.'

Also, I was now realising that my childish stories that had captured the attention of my friends now cut little ice with the big boys of the story world.

My typewriter ribbon was also threadbare and I had to replace it. This took a lot of pushing and pulling until I got it into position. And if some of my friends muttered, when seeing my blue fingers, about being fingerprinted, then that was their problem. They weren't the ones having to read the typewriter manual, which could have been written in Cantonese for all the good it did me.

Also, I was too busy with the correction fluid and I think there should be an evening class showing the best way to use this wonderful liquid. I could never get the hang of it and instead of omitting one wrong word, I would end up omitting half a page.

I often thought back to the happy, innocent time

when I imagined writing to be easy. How could I have been so wrong?

Writing is a bit like show business. It's an overcrowded profession and for every one who makes the big time, there are hundreds of hopefuls pouring out their stories with plots of murder, love, humour and mayhem; all of us dreaming of becoming another writing genius.

After years of rejection slips, I often thought of taking a leaf out of Barbra Streisand's film, *Funny Girl*, climbing to the top of the highest building and singing:

'Hey, Mr Publisher, here I am.'